THE MAKING OF
DONALD
TRUMP

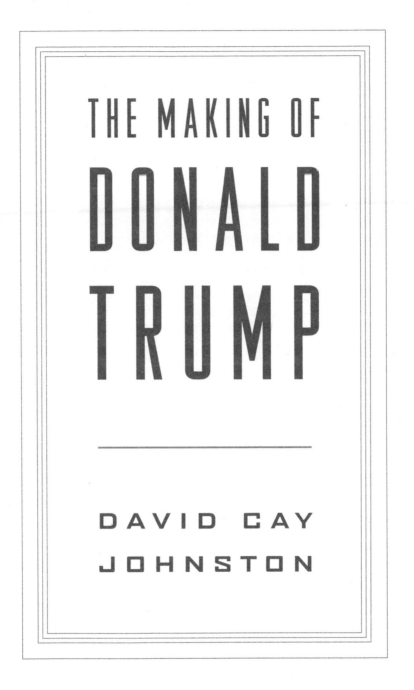

THE MAKING OF
DONALD
TRUMP

DAVID CAY JOHNSTON

MELVILLE HOUSE
BROOKLYN • LONDON

THE MAKING OF DONALD TRUMP

First Melville House Printing: August 2016

"Old Man Trump." Words by Woody Guthrie, music by Ryan Harvey.
© Woody Guthrie Publications, Inc. (BMI) & Ryan Harvey (ASCAP).
All rights reserved. Used by permission.

Melville House Publishing		8 Blackstock Mews
46 John Street	and	Islington
Brooklyn, NY 11201		London N4 2BT

mhpbooks.com   facebook.com/mhpbooks   @melvillehouse

ISBN: 978-1-61219-632-9

Design by Fritz Metsch

Printed in the United States of America
3   5   7   9   10   8   6   4

A catalog record for this book is available
from the Library of Congress

For

Gene Roberts and Glenn Kramon, editors

and

John Wasserburger, teacher

CONTENTS

INTRODUCTION

When Donald Trump rode down the Trump Tower lobby escalator live on national television in June 2015 to announce his campaign for president, nearly every journalist treated his candidacy as a vanity project. Not me.

I have been an investigative reporter since I was eighteen years old. I've been digging up facts, getting laws changed, and generally making a lot of trouble reporting for the *San Jose Mercury*, the *Detroit Free Press*, the *Los Angeles Times*, *The Philadelphia Inquirer*, and finally for *The New York Times*.

From the start, I acted on my own authority in deciding what to report. I was a newsroom rogue who got away with it because my stories engaged readers and got big results: a broadcast chain forced off the air for news manipulations; an innocent man saved from life in prison after I confronted the real killer; Jack Welch giving up his retirement perks; political spying and crimes by the Los Angeles Police Department revealed, along with foreign agents secretly interfering in American politics. While at my last paper, I won a Pulitzer Prize for exposing so many tax dodges and loopholes that a prominent tax law professor called me the "de facto chief tax enforcement officer of the United States."

In 1987, I got interested in casinos after the Supreme Court ruled that Native Americans had a right to own them. I was sure it would lead to the spread of casinos across the country—casinos run mostly by corporate America. For the only time in my life, I applied for a job. *The Philadelphia Inquirer* liked my idea: in June 1988, I moved to Atlantic City.

A few days later, I met Donald Trump.

I sized him up as a modern P. T. Barnum selling tickets to a modern variation of the Feejee Mermaid, one of the panoply of Barnum's famous fakes that people decided were worth a bit of their money. Trump was full of himself. I quickly learned from others in town that he knew next to nothing about the casino industry, including the rules of the games. That would turn out to be important, as explained in two chapters near the end of this book.

In the nearly thirty years since then, I have followed Trump intensely; I've paid close attention to his business dealings and I've interviewed him multiple times. In 1990, I broke the story that, instead of being worth billions, as he'd claimed, Trump actually had a negative net worth and escaped a chaotic collapse into personal bankruptcy only when the government took his side over the bank's, as you will read.

Before technology allowed me to digitize files, I built up a vast trove of Trump documents, as investigative reporters often do with subjects that interest them. I had so many Bankers Boxes of files on Trump and other prominent Americans—Barron Hilton, Jack Welch, and Los Angeles police chief

Daryl Gates among them—that for years I rented two storage lockers just to hold them all.

So when Trump announced his bid for the Republican nomination for the 2016 election, I knew it was for real. I'd spent decades reporting on him and I had kept my files. In addition, reporter Wayne Barrett had generously shared his.

First, I knew that Trump has been talking about the presidency since 1985. In 1988, he proposed himself as the running mate of the first President George Bush, a job that went to Senator Dan Quayle. In July of the same year, I watched him arrive in Atlantic City on his yacht, the *Trump Princess*, where cheering crowds greeted him. A phalanx of teenage girls, jumping up and down, squealed with delight as if they had just seen their favorite rock star. As Trump and his then wife, Ivana, took an escalator up into his Trump's Castle Casino, a crowd cheered him on. One man shouted loudly, "Be our president, Donald!"

I also watched Trump run in 2000 on the ticket for the Reform Party, a fringe group with members in the tens of thousands (as opposed to the millions who call themselves Democrats or Republicans). It was during that brief campaign that Trump declared he would become the first person to run for president and make a profit. He said he had a million-dollar deal to give ten speeches at motivational speaking events hosted by Tony Robbins. He coordinated his campaign appearances around them so the campaign would pay for the use of his Boeing 727 jet. It was classic Trump, seeing profit in everything, even politics. Few people knew about it.

For the 2016 run as well, a large share of Trump's campaign money has been spent paying himself for the use of his Boeing 757, his smaller jet, his helicopter, his Trump Tower office space, and other services supplied by Trump businesses. By law, Trump must pay charter rates for his aircraft and market prices for services from his other businesses. This anticorruption law was designed to prevent vendors from underpricing services to win political favors—a legacy of a time when no one imagined that a man of Trump's presumed immense wealth would buy campaign services from himself. In 2016, the law ensures that Trump makes a profit from his campaign.

Trump again declared his candidacy in 2012. He was treated as a serious contender by just about everyone except Lawrence O'Donnell of MSNBC and me. Separately, O'Donnell and I both came to the conclusion that Trump's campaign then had a purpose other than moving to 1600 Pennsylvania Avenue. His real goal, we surmised, was a more lucrative contract with the NBC television network for his aging *Celebrity Apprentice* show, where his trademark line was "You're fired."

Indeed, when Trump dropped out, he said, in effect, that as much as the country needed him in the White House, his show needed him more. Based on that, journalists concluded his campaign had been a strange joke. As such, they gave little regard to his announcement for the 2016 election.

But this time things were different. Trump's ratings were in decline. His show was at risk of being canceled. To Trump, a man who reads the New York tabloids religiously, I knew that just about the worst fate he could imagine for himself, short of death, would be waking up to these *Daily News* and *Post* covers: "NBC to Trump: You're Fired."

As soon as Trump announced in 2015, I immediately set out to report what the mainstream news media were not. I wrote an early piece that posed twenty-one questions I thought reporters should ask on the campaign trail. Not one of them did. Late in the primaries, Senator Marco Rubio brought up my question about Trump University and Senator Ted Cruz posed my question about Trump's dealings with the Genovese and Gambino crime families, matters explored in this book. I will always wonder what might have happened had journalists and some of the sixteen candidates vying with Trump for the Republican nomination started asking my questions months earlier.

This book is my effort to make sure Americans know a fuller story about Trump than the one he has polished and promoted with such exceptional skill and determination. Trump, who presents himself as a modern Midas even when much of what he touches turns to dross, has studied the conventions of journalists and displays more genius at exploiting them to his advantage than anyone else I have ever known.

More important, Trump has worked just as hard to make sure few people know about his lifelong entanglements with a major cocaine trafficker, with mobsters and many mob associates, with con artists and swindlers. He has been sued thousands of times for refusing to pay employees, vendors, and others. Investors have sued him for fraud in a number of different cities. But among Trump's most highly refined skills is his ability to deflect or shut down law enforcement investigations. He also uses threats of litigation to deter news organizations from looking behind the curtain of the seemingly all-wise and all-powerful man they often refer to as The Donald.

At one of my first meetings with Trump, I did something I hope many journalists will do before the November 2016 elections. I brought up a casino issue that Trump did not know much about, intentionally saying something that was false, a technique that has many uses in investigative reporting. Trump immediately embraced my faux fact and shaped his answer to it, much the way television psychics listen for clues in what people say to shape their soothsaying.

Trump's habit of picking up on what others say was on full display when Lester Holt, the NBC *Nightly News* anchor, asked Trump in late June 2016 about his claim that Hillary Clinton had slept through the Benghazi attack. After Holt noted it had been mid-afternoon where Clinton was, Trump tried to incorporate that into his answer, then tried to bluff his way out of not knowing the facts.

For those who doubt that Trump lacks basic knowledge about important issues, I will provide many examples. Here is one to set the stage:

During the Republican presidential debate hosted by CNN in December 2015, the conservative radio talk show host Hugh Hewitt asked Trump, "What's your priority among our nuclear triad?"

"Well, first of all, I think we need somebody absolutely that we can trust, who is totally responsible, who really knows what he or she is doing," Trump responded. "That is so powerful and so important. And one of the things that I'm frankly most proud of is that in 2003, 2004, I was totally against going into Iraq because you're going to destabilize the Middle East. I called it. I called it very strongly. And it was very important. But we have to be extremely vigilant and extremely careful when it comes to nuclear. Nuclear changes the whole ball game. Frankly, I would have said get out of Syria; get out—if we didn't have the power of weaponry today. The power is so massive that we can't just leave areas that fifty years ago or seventy-five years ago we wouldn't care [about]. It was hand-to-hand combat . . ."

Hewitt then followed up, asking, "Of the three legs of the triad, though, do you have a priority?"

Trump responded: "I think—I think, for me, nuclear is just the power, the devastation is very important to me."

Hewitt then turned to Senator Marco Rubio of Florida, whom Trump often derided as an empty suit. "Do you have a response?"

"First, let's explain to people at home what the triad is," Rubio said. "The triad is our ability in the United States to conduct nuclear attacks using airplanes, using missiles launched from silos or from the ground, or from our nuclear subs."

This was not the first time Trump had been asked about how he would allocate money among the three different methods by which the United States military can deliver nuclear bombs. Four months earlier, Hewitt had asked Trump the same question on his radio show. Trump gave an answer indicating he had no idea what Hewitt was asking about. He had clearly made no effort in the intervening months to learn.

"I think one of the most important things that we have to worry about is nuclear generally speaking," Trump said on Hewitt's radio show. "The power of nuclear, the power of the weapons that we have today—and that is, by the way, the deal with Iran—the concept of it is so important that you have to make a good deal and what they should have done is that they should have doubled up and tripled up the sanctions . . ."

This book is a presentation of the facts as I have witnessed them and as the public record shows. They are facts reported with the same flint-eyed diligence as everything else I have written about in the past half century.

Many have asked why I'm not writing a book about Hillary Clinton instead of, or as well as, writing a book about Donald Trump. The answer is that in 1988 I wound up in Atlantic City instead of Arkansas. I know Trump; I have never spoken to Clinton or her husband. However, as first lady she was furious over my *New York Times* articles revealing that she and her husband paid more than twice as much income tax as the law required because, despite paying almost $10,000 a year to have their tax returns prepared, they got bad tax advice.

One last thing to keep in mind as you read this book: those applauding crowds of young people who filled the Trump Tower auditorium in June 2015 when Trump announced his campaign with vicious denunciations of Mexicans, Muslims, and the media. At the time, I thought that was incongruous for midtown Manhattan, a place not exactly known for xeno-phobia or applause for racist tirades. Indeed, that crowd was not the voluntary outpouring that television viewers would reasonably have believed they were seeing. Many of those clapping were actors paid fifty bucks apiece.

THE MAKING OF
DONALD
TRUMP

1

—

FAMILY HISTORY

The Trump family's deep roots in Germany stretch back to the war-ravaged seventeenth century, when the family name was Drumpf. In 1648, they simplified the name to one that would prove to be a powerful brand for their latter-day descendants.

Looking back from the twenty-first century, it turns out to have been an interesting choice. Donald no doubt enjoys the bridge player's definition of *trump*: a winning play by a card that outranks all others. But other definitions include "a thing of small value, a trifle" and "to deceive or cheat" as well as "to blow or sound a trumpet." As a verb, *trump* means "to devise in an unscrupulous way" and "to forge, fabricate or invent," as in "trumped-up" charges.

Donald Trump never knew his grandfather, Friedrich, who died when Donald's father, Fred, was only twelve years old. As a rogue entrepreneur, however, Friedrich cast a century-long shadow over the Trump family with his passion for money and the flouting of legal niceties—such as erecting buildings on land he did not own.

Friedrich Trump grew up in the winemaking region of southwest Germany, in the town of Kallstadt, where hard work meant a roof over one's head, not riches. His father had died when Friedrich was only eight years old. In 1885, at the age of sixteen and facing mandatory military service, Friedrich left his mother a note and did what millions of other Europeans with few prospects at home were doing: fled Germany for the United States.

Enduring a surely difficult North Atlantic crossing in a packed steamship, Friedrich eventually landed in New York, where he moved in with an older sister, Katherine, and her husband, both of whom had immigrated earlier.

Before long, the young man decided to go west, eventually settling in Seattle, where he opened The Dairy Restaurant. It also had a curtained-off area that most likely served as a low-rent whorehouse, according to Gwenda Blair, who had the family's cooperation in her history of the Trumps.

In 1892, Friedrich became a citizen, lying about his age in the process by saying he'd landed in New York two years before he actually had. Two friends accompanied him to the proceedings to attest to his good character. One was a laborer, the other a man whose occupations included providing accommodations for what Blair politely called "female boarding."

Friedrich was the genesis of many Trump family traditions in America, but voting was not among them. In fact, his grandson Donald would run for president after failing to vote in the 2002 general election and, as records indicate, in any Republican primary from 1989 until he voted for himself in 2016. Friedrich's great-grandchildren were even less diligent in their civic duties. When Donald Trump's name appeared on the New York State primary ballot in 2016, his daughter Ivanka and son Eric, both in their thirties, could not cast ballots because they had neglected to register as Republicans. They blamed the government, saying they should have been allowed to change from independent to Republican at the last minute. But the primary voting rules, however outmoded, had been law in the Empire State for many years. The siblings had months in which to change their registration so they could vote for their father.

A family tradition Friedrich Trump did start in America, however, was the art of prospering but wanting more. Friedrich sold his restaurant/bordello and set up a new business about thirty miles north. Rumor had it that the oil-rich Rockefellers planned a big mining operation in the area. On a piece of land he didn't own, right across from the train station, Friedrich built a hotel of sorts—one intended mostly for, shall we say, active short stays, not overnight visits. Building on land he did not own foreshadowed the terms under which his grandson Donald would acquire the Florida mansion Mar-a-Lago: with a mortgage that Chase Bank agreed in writing not to record at the courthouse.

In the end, the mining project fizzled and only a few got out better off than they were when they arrived. Among them was Friedrich Trump, who had, by that point, Americanized his name to Frederick. He went by Fred.

Hearing about the Klondike gold rush, Frederick headed for Canada's Yukon Territory. He had no interest in the hard physical labor of panning for gold in frigid streams; Frederick mined the miners. He built a sort of bar and grill, calling the joint The Arctic. It offered hard liquor and "sporting ladies," as the prostitutes were called. Again his timing was impeccable. He arrived when the gold rush was at its height. By the time the gold was running out and the Royal Canadian Mounted Police were riding in, Fred Trump had made a small fortune to take with him as he skedaddled back to America.

In 1901, at age thirty-two, Frederick Trump returned to Germany, where his mother introduced her now-rich son to eligible young ladies. Frederick, however, took a liking to a woman his mother did not care for, a twenty-year-old blonde named Elizabeth Christ. Just six years old when her husband-to-be had slipped away to America to avoid the German draft, Elizabeth had grown into a well-endowed adulthood. Trump men favoring busty blondes would become a family pattern.

Frederick took his new bride to America and scouted for opportunities to increase his fortune, by then worth a half million dollars or so in today's money. But Elizabeth had no love for bustling New York and its stark contrasts between wealth and want. She desperately wanted to go home. In 1904, Frederick, with his young wife and their infant daughter, sailed back to Germany.

Once there, however, he had to convince the authorities to overlook his draft dodging. Hoping the fortune he brought into the country would impress the authorities, in September 1904 he explained his absence to the government in writing: "I did not immigrate to America in order to avoid military service, but to establish for myself a profitable livelihood and to enable myself to support my mother" in Kallstadt. German authorities didn't buy it; they ordered him to leave.

Donald Trump has not yet been asked whether this episode of family history plays any role in his unconstitutional proposals to deport an estimated eleven million immigrants who entered the country illegally, including those whose children are American citizens, or if he thinks of it when suggesting that the United States block soldiers and sailors who are Muslim from returning to America.

Back in New York City, Frederick continued to prosper. In her richly detailed biography, Gwenda Blair suggests Frederick worked as a barber, a low-paid occupation that seems odd for a man so focused on making money. She notes that barbershops also sold tobacco in those days, but that was still a low-paying opportunity. However, they were often fronts for illegal businesses and—because men of dubious means could come in for a daily shave or just to hang out—they could also have been opportune places to gather business intelligence and engage in sub rosa transactions with the many ethnic criminal elements in the big city.

Whatever he was up to, Frederick's fortune couldn't buy him more time: he became one of the more than twenty million people around the world who died during the 1918 influenza pandemic. He was followed by another industrious Trump: Donald's father, Fred.

2

—

FAMILY VALUES

Though only twelve years old when his father died in 1918, a mere two years later Frederick Christ Trump took after his father by starting a residential garage–building company with his mother: Elizabeth Trump & Son. Elizabeth had to sign all the checks and documents because her ambitious boy was still a teenager not legally allowed to enter into contracts.

Fred Trump entered his majority by getting himself arrested at age twenty-one for his involvement in a battle between about a hundred New York City police officers and a thousand Ku Klux Klan members and supporters, many of them in white robes. The riot took place in Jamaica, the Queens neighborhood where Fred Trump lived. Police booked him for failure to disperse, but prosecutors later declined to try him and many of the others arrested that day. It was the first of many indications of Fred Trump's racial enmity.

Almost nine decades later, his son Donald, running for president, tried to deny the whole thing, claiming his father never lived at the address the newspapers had obtained from police records. Other public records verify that it was indeed his father's address. They also show only one Fred Trump living in Queens during that period.

Cornered in a 2015 interview with *The New York Times*, Donald Trump bobbed, weaved, and tried to persuade the paper to ignore the arrest, which the website boingboing.net had written about after uncovering a 1927 *New York Times* article about it. Trump's comments went like this:

> It never happened. And they said there were no charges, no nothing. It's unfair to mention it, to be honest, because there were no charges. They said there were charges against other people, but there were absolutely no charges, totally false . . . Somebody showed me that website—it was a little website and somebody did that. By the way, did you notice that there were no charges? Well, if there are no charges that means it shouldn't be mentioned . . . Because my father, there were no charges against him, I don't know about the other people involved. But there were zero charges against him. So assuming it was him—I don't even think it was him, I never even heard about it. So it's really not fair to mention. It never happened . . . if there are no charges that means it shouldn't be mentioned.

That last line is important to understanding the gap between what is widely reported about Trump and what the public record indisputably shows: that events not resulting in criminal charges should not be mentioned in the news has been a major theme in Donald Trump's careful and consistent efforts to limit inquiries into his conduct. His wealth and public prominence are closely tied to his success in focusing the attention of journalists where he wants it and his skill in deflecting inquiries by law enforcement and people suing him for alleged civil fraud or failure to make payments, as we shall see.

In any event, as the Roaring Twenties came to an end, Fred Trump was building single-family houses in Queens. When the Great Depression began in 1929, he switched to opening a self-service grocery. It was a precursor to the modern supermarket, cutting costs because people picked their own goods off the shelf, eliminating the need for most clerks. The business was a smashing success, and Trump sold it for a substantial profit after a year.

During World War II, Fred Trump landed government contracts for apartments and barracks to be built near Navy shipyards in Pennsylvania and Virginia. From this he learned the ins and outs of government procurement, a skill he would put to profitable use after the war ended. When the federal government started financing postwar housing for returning GIs, Fred Trump was said to have been the first builder to show up with his papers at the Federal Housing Administration loan counter in Washington. In the years that followed, he would build many thousands of apartments in Brooklyn and Queens and would buy other apartments as far away as Ohio.

Fred Trump was known neither for quality buildings nor for being a good landlord. He bought the cheapest materials to build more than 27,000 subsidized apartments and row houses, on many of which his family continues to collect rent decades later.

He was also something of a showman, displaying the panache his son would later take to dazzling extremes. Fred the Brooklyn Builder knew just how to spin the kind of simple, telling tale that newspapers often embrace without deep fact-checking. For example, in 1946 he told the *Brooklyn Eagle* that because building supplies were so hard to come by after the war, he'd had his men visit hardware stores across the city and beyond to buy all the nails they could find, even if they could only procure a handful. Later, he became known for a frugal habit: when he showed up at his construction sites (always dressed in a tailored suit and tie), he would bend down to pick up loose nails and hand them to carpenters.

Years later came a stunt that would appear to be a direct inspiration to his son: While under intense criticism for plans to destroy a popular Coney Island attraction, the Steeplechase amusement ride, where he wanted to build the first apartment project bearing the family name, Fred Trump shifted the focus of news coverage by hiring a bevy of beauties in hard hats and polka-dot bikinis to hand out bricks to locals and city dignitaries. Then he summoned news photographers to watch them all throw the bricks at the symbol of the ride, a stained-glass icon called the Funny Face. Decades later, of course, Donald Trump would surround himself with models to attract television cameras and would have his third wife pose nearly nude aboard his Boeing 757 jet for a men's magazine while he looked on during the photo shoot.

Long before he learned to manufacture news, Fred Trump had become a main target of federal investigators looking into profiteering with the tax dollars intended to help World War II veterans. The subsequent Senate hearings about those investigations were not about diversionary tactics like young women in bikinis with bricks, but the fortunes Trump and other builders made by gaming Federal Housing Administration rules on mortgage guarantees. Once the FHA understood the scheme, it was explained to President Dwight D. Eisenhower, who reportedly flew into a rage in the Oval Office. Soon the FHA had more than a hundred investigators combing through bureaucratic records, comparing costs to profits and discovering huge gaps between the numbers.

On July 13, 1954, the *Brooklyn Eagle* ran a banner headline, "Denies $4 Million Profit," and above it a kicker: "But Trump has that much surplus in bank." Trump was already a household name, at least in Brooklyn.

Testifying before the Senate Committee on Banking and Currency, Fred Trump insisted that he had not made an excess profit of nearly $4 million, as the investigative report said. Trump said it was all a misunderstanding, but his explanation employed a view of finance that does not exist in any textbook or accounting manual: Trump said the money was there, for sure, sitting in the bank account for his FHA-subsidized projects, but it was wrong to describe this as profiteering—indeed, it was not even profit, he said, *because he had not taken any of that money out of the bank.*

This description was, to anyone who understood finance, absurd. His son Donald would also use creative approaches in fostering the impression that he had earned billions of dollars through his deal-making artistry.

Fred Trump testified before Congress that the reasons he had nearly $4 million in the bank were lower costs for materials than he had expected, a faster completion of the construction, and the fact that he acted as his own general contractor. That fit with his reputation as a builder who got things done and ahead of schedule, though the schedules often had lots of slack built in, making an early finish easy. Fred then did his best to turn the tables, attacking the investigators for, he said, doing "untold damage to my standing and reputation." There was talk of perjury indictments, but nothing ever came of the FHA investigation.

A month after Fred Trump's testimony in Washington, merchants in the Fort Greene area of Brooklyn complained that Trump, backed by federal slum-clearance money to take over their neighborhood, had gouged them on rent. Store-keepers told the *Brooklyn Eagle* that he was doubling rents, which was "immoral."

Adopting the same stance he had on Capitol Hill, Fred Trump said it was all just a misunderstanding. The merchants had been paying vastly different rents for similar proper-ties—$40 a month for one storefront, $200 for another—which Fred Trump said made no sense. He also said that he expected the merchants to be out within a couple of years so he could build a new apartment project using the slum-clearance powers the government had enacted . . . and from which he would soon profit.

Taxpayers were not the only source of capital for Fred Trump's construction projects. A few years after the war ended, he took on a partner known as Willie Tomasello. When cash was short, Tomasello was able to provide Trump with operating capital on short notice. Tomasello also saw to it that there was no trouble from the unions, from the brick-layers and carpenters to the teamsters.

The New York State Organized Crime Task Force identi-fied Tomasello as an associate of the Genovese and Gambino Mafia families in New York. In other words, just as Friedrich Trump had engaged in illicit businesses to build his fortune in the late nineteeth century, his son Fred Trump turned to an organized crime associate as his longtime partner to build his own. Decades later, Donald Trump would also do business with the heads of the same families, though at a remove, developing numerous business connections with an assortment of criminals, from con artists and a major drug trafficker to the heads of the two largest Mafia families in New York City, as we shall see.

It should be no surprise that Donald Trump took after his father. Fred Christ Trump was a stern father who expected his sons to learn the family business. He had his oldest son, Fred Jr., and the younger boys, Donald and then Robert, learn the business from the ground up, actually driving them regularly to his properties in his blue Cadillac. (He bought a new one every two years. It had what at the time was a novelty, a customized license plate reading "FCT".) The boys were assigned to sweep out storage rooms, empty coins from the basement washers and dryers, make minor repairs under the supervision of maintenance crews, and, as they got a little older, collect rents.

It was not that the boys needed the little bit of money Dad gave them for their labors. When Donald was still in diapers, he and his siblings had a trust fund. His share was about $12,000 a year, which in the late nineteen forties was roughly four times the typical income for a married couple with children if the husband held a full-time job.

Fred worked out of an austere Avenue Z office in Brooklyn, assisted by a secretary who stayed with him for more than a half century. (He told others it was best to hire an overweight and unattractive secretary because she would stay on the job.)

I've talked with people who sat across from Fred's plain desk, proposing to do plumbing, window, and electrical work. They describe a ritual that was certainly not unique to that office. First, a plain envelope would be presented. Fred would take a second to test its weight in his hand before putting it into a drawer. Then he would listen to the pitch about contract terms for work on his buildings.

The cost of these secretive extras was built into the contract cost when it could be passed on to Uncle Sam or tenants. Otherwise it reduced the profit the contractor made. This was, and remains today, a widespread but illegal practice unless the cash payments are reported on income tax returns—which of course would defeat the purpose of the inducements. It's a low-risk crime: Unless the party handing over the envelope is a government agent and the bills are marked, who's to know? The practice also meant there was little need to withdraw cash from bank accounts, thereby leaving no records for tax authorities to discover during an audit.

As first-born, Fred Jr. was first in line to rise in dad's business. Neither the work nor his father's methods appealed, apparently. Fred Sr. was a no-nonsense businessman who watched every penny, kept regular hours, and, after dinner at home each night, resumed doing business on the telephone. Fred Jr. was more of a free, albeit troubled, spirit. He went off in a Corvette to Lehigh University in Bethlehem, Pennsylvania, and learned to fly airplanes. Although he was not Jewish, he said he was in order to join the Jewish fraternity.

When Fred Jr. tried working for his namesake early on, the father and son did not see the landlord business the same way. For example, when Fred Jr. bought new windows for one of the Trump apartment houses instead of having the old ones repaired, his father upbraided him for wasting money. In recounting this episode years later, Donald said his father freely dispensed criticism, but rarely praise. Donald said that was just fine with him, but not his older brother.

Donald was what school counselors might call "maladjusted." In his first book, *The Art of the Deal*, he boasts about slugging his music teacher in second grade because he didn't think the teacher knew the subject, although the story might be apocryphal. Neighbors have told stories over the years, including to me, of a child Donald throwing rocks at little children in playpens and provoking disputes with other kids. By his own account, Donald got into lots of trouble—so much that his father shipped him off to the New York Military Academy in upstate New York to develop discipline when he was a teenager.

Donald turned eighteen in 1964, when the death toll in Vietnam was rising fast. He got four student deferments and one medical deferment after his doctor wrote that he had a bone spur in his foot. Which foot? a journalist asked years later. Trump said he could not recall. He was accepted into a Catholic school in New York City, Fordham College, but in his junior year transferred to an Ivy League school, the University of Pennsylvania in Philadelphia. Penn has a famous and highly regarded graduate business school that Trump often invokes. He did not in fact study there. He was enrolled as an undergraduate and received a bachelor of science in economics.

While in college, Donald also started doing real estate deals, including one with his father in Cincinnati. He later wrote that his net worth upon graduating from college was $200,000, a figure that seems modest given the amount of money that had been flowing into his trust fund since before he learned how to walk.

Meanwhile, Fred Jr. had become a pilot for TWA. He married a flight attendant whom family members describe simultaneously as being a knockout in the looks department and yet someone whom Fred Sr. couldn't stand—just as his paternal grandmother couldn't stand Elizabeth Christ Trump, the woman his father, Friedrich, had married. Fred Jr. and his wife, Linda, subsequently had two children and divorced. Afterward, Fred Jr. gave up flying when he couldn't manage his alcoholism.

With the way now open to becoming next in line in the family business, Donald, even before graduating from college, started modeling himself more directly after his father. He drove a Cadillac with the license plate "DJT." He took a flashy Penn student, the actress Candice Bergen, on a dinner date that ended early. The only thing she remembered years later was that Trump wore a three-piece burgundy suit with matching leather boots.

Others have said they don't recall seeing Trump a lot around campus, an interesting observation in view of Trump's claims years later that "nobody remembers seeing" future President Barack Obama in elementary school in Hawaii or anywhere else. In fact, many of Obama's fellow students have spoken and written about him, as have several of his professors, notably constitutional scholar Laurence Tribe. While Obama was still a first-year law student, Tribe wrote a law review article citing Obama in the first footnote. Tribe has since written about how Obama sat in the front row in every session, offering nuanced legal analyses that Tribe remembered because of his student's ability to examine a subtle legal issue from the perspective of each relevant party with equal weight.

Nonetheless, Trump touts his 1968 bachelor's degree in economics and says he learned "super genius stuff" at the University of Pennsylvania's Wharton School. "I was a really good student at the best school," Trump told Barbara Walters on her show, *The View*. "I'm like a smart guy."

Wharton, like all business schools, teaches fundamental tools for evaluating whether investments are likely to be profitable. One such concept is Net Present Value, or NPV. That is the value of cash expected from an investment minus the value spent to support that investment and then reduced to a lump sum payable today. Business and finance graduates of Ivy League schools know this concept the way primary school students know that 2+2=4.

In a lawsuit Trump filed against journalist Timothy L. O'Brien for writing that Trump's net worth may be far less than a billion dollars, a lawyer asked Trump questions about his knowledge of finance and how he determined his net worth.

"Are you familiar with the concept of net present value?" lawyer Andrew Ceresney asked.

"The concept of net present value to me," Trump replied, "would be the value of the land currently after debt. Well, to me, the word 'net' is an interesting word. It's really—the word 'value' is the important word. If you have an asset that you can do other things with but you don't choose to do them—I haven't chosen to do that."

After hearing that gibberish, the lawyer asked Trump to explain another basic business concept taught to finance students: generally accepted accounting principles, or GAAP. Did he understand GAAP? "No," Trump said. "I'm not an accountant."

Once out of college, Donald Trump set his sights not just on finding young women in need of a man with a fortune, but also on establishing his name across the East River in Manhattan, where the bright lights beckoned. Less than sixteen years later, he would erect on Fifth Avenue the first building bearing his name in big, bronze letters.

3

—

PERSONAL VALUES

I n 2005, Donald Trump flew to Colorado to give a motivational talk. Accompanying him were his wife, Melania, and a violent convicted felon and swindler named Felix Sater, who was helping Trump make two major development deals in Denver. Trump and Sater gave interviews to the *Rocky Mountain News*—interviews that would prove to be significant a few years later. The three took a limousine an hour north to Loveland, solidly Republican territory where more than a thousand people had paid to hear Trump's advice on how to succeed in life and business.

Motivational speakers like Zig Ziglar and Tony Robbins work up audiences with carefully crafted talks. They make lofty appeals to people about vanquishing inner demons so a better self can flourish and dreams of success can morph into reality.

Trump's talk was nothing like that.

For more than an hour, Trump let fly one four-letter expletive after another. He had no prepared text, much less a rehearsed presentation. He ripped into the location and functionality of the Denver International Airport. The rambling remarks were rich with denunciations of former wives and former business associates. In vilifying a former employee, saying she had been disloyal, Trump gratuitously described her as "ugly as a dog."

"I have to tell you about losers," Trump told the audience. "I love losers because they make me feel so good about myself." Had Loveland's Bixpo 2005 conference invited a loser to speak, he assured the crowd, the fee would have been three dollars rather than the "freaking fortune" paid to Trump. However large the speaking fee had been, it did not motivate Trump to show enough respect for the paying audience to prepare even a simple outline. Many in the crowd said afterward that none of his talk was useful and certainly not uplifting.

However, within Trump's inchoate vitriol, some in the audience did identify two recommendations on how to succeed in life and business:

First, Trump advised, trust no one, especially good employees. "Be paranoid," he said, "because they are gonna try to fleece you." It was strange advice, as some in the audience told local reporters afterward, because trust is central to market capitalism. Businesspeople known for being trustworthy attract better workers, who in turn make their businesses run better. Trustworthy entrepreneurs make the economy more efficient by reducing friction in business deals. Business owners who are prudent about making promises and are known for honoring their word often go through life without a single lawsuit. Trump has been a party in more than 3,500 lawsuits, some of them accusing him of civil fraud (an issue we will examine in another chapter).

Second, Trump recommended revenge as business policy. "Get even," he said. "If somebody screws you, you screw 'em back ten times over. At least you can feel good about it. Boy, do I feel good."

Two years after the Loveland speech, Trump released *Think Big*, his twelfth book. *Think Big* was coauthored by Bill Zanker, founder of The Learning Annex, which runs classes on everything from pole dancing and making your own soap to writing business plans. Chapter 6 of *Think Big* is titled "Revenge."

"I always get even," Trump writes in the opening line of that chapter. He then launches into an attack on the same woman he had denounced in Colorado. Trump recruited the unnamed woman "from her government job where she was making peanuts"; her career going nowhere. "I decided to make her somebody. I gave her a great job at the Trump Organization, and over time she became powerful in real estate. She bought a beautiful home."

When Trump was in financial trouble in the early 1990s, "I asked her to make a phone call to an extremely close friend of hers who held a powerful position at a big bank and who would have done what she asked. She said, 'Donald, I can't do that.'" Instead of accepting that the woman felt such a call would be improper, Trump fired her. She started her own business. Trump writes that her business failed. "I was really happy when I found that out," he says.

In Trump's telling, the story of an employee declining to do something unseemly is really the story of a rebellion to be crushed.

She has turned on me after I had done so much to help her. I had asked her for one favor in return and she turned me down flat. She ended up losing her home. Her husband, who was only in it for the money, walked out on her and I was glad. Over the years many people have called asking for a recommendation for her. I only gave her bad recommendations. I can't stomach disloyalty . . . and now I go out of my way to make her life miserable.

Trump devotes another several pages to actress Rosie O'Donnell, who described him as "a snake-oil salesman" in 2006. A few months later, at Zanker's 2007 Learning Annex Real Estate & Wealth Expo, Trump called O'Donnell "a pig," "a degenerate," "a slob," and later (on television) "disgusting inside and out." He made disparaging remarks about her looks, weight, and sexuality and said on national television that O'Donnell's emotional health would improve if she never looked in a mirror.

In *Think Big*, Trump calls O'Donnell a bully: "You've got to hit a bully really hard really strongly, right between the eyes . . . [I] hit that horrible woman right smack in the middle of the eyes. It's true . . . some people would have ignored her insults. I decided to fight back and make her regret the day she decided to unload on me!"

At the end of the chapter, Trump writes, "I love getting even when I get screwed by someone—yes, it is true . . . Always get even. When you are in business you need to get even with people who screw you. You need to screw them back fifteen times harder . . . go for the jugular, attack them in spades!"

Trump's words take on more significance when read in the context of his campaign statement, "No one reads the Bible more than I do." He says *The Art of the Deal* is the greatest book ever written except for the Bible. He has never been able to recite a biblical verse.

Among the many biblical verses warning against vengeance is Romans 12:19, which in one modern translation
states, "Do not take revenge, my dear friends, but leave room
for God's wrath, for it is written: 'It is mine to avenge; I will
repay,' says the Lord."

Just before the New York State primary election in April
2016, Trump told Bob Lonsberry, a radio host in Rochester,
New York, that he was religious. "Is there a favorite Bible
verse or favorite story that has informed your thinking or
character?" Lonsberry asked.

"Well, I think many," Trump replied. "I mean, when we
get into the Bible, I think many, so many. And some people—
look, an eye for an eye, you can almost say that. That's not a
particularly nice thing. But you know, if you look at what's
happening to our country, I mean, when you see what's going
on with our country, how people are taking advantage of
us . . . we have to be firm and have to be very strong. And we
can learn a lot from the Bible, that I can tell you."

His invocation of "an eye for an eye" alludes to Exodus
21:24. But Trump, who made a show of attending Presbyterian
services once during the campaign, seemed unaware that, in
the Sermon on the Mount, Jesus repudiated this Old Testament verse, saying in one modern translation:

But I tell you, do not resist an evil person. If anyone slaps
you on the right cheek, turn to them the other cheek
also. And if anyone wants to sue you and take your
shirt, hand over your coat as well. If anyone forces you
to go one mile, go with them two miles. Give to the one
who asks you, and do not turn away from the one who
wants to borrow from you.

You have heard that it was said, "Love your neighbor

and hate your enemy." But I tell you, love your enemies
and pray for those who persecute you, that you may be
children of your Father in heaven . . . (Matthew 5:39–45)

Sixteen pages of *Think Big* are devoted to revenge. All of
them run directly contrary to this basic biblical teaching.
Trump leaves no room for doubt that revenge is a guiding
principle of his life—"My motto is: Always get even. When
someone screws you, get them back in spades"—but that
guiding principle stands in direct opposition to both Christian
and Jewish theology.

On another page of *Think Big*, Trump acknowledges that
"this is not your typical advice, get even, but this is real-life
advice. If you don't get even, you are just a schmuck! I really
mean it, too." It will come as no surprise that Trump's views
on revenge were not limited to employees he considered disloyal, people he had done deals with, or even petty insults by
an actress. In fact, in the year 2000, Trump turned his revenge
on his own family.

4

—

A SICKLY CHILD

wo of Donald Trump's mottos, "Always get even" and "Hit back harder than you were hit," came into play shortly after his father died in 1999 at the age of ninety-three. More than six hundred people filled Marble Collegiate Church in Manhattan, far from the outer boroughs where Fred Sr. had lived and owned apartments. Among those speaking was his namesake grandson, Fred Trump III, Donald's nephew, son of Fred Jr. He described his grandfather as a generous man who always took care of others. The next day, Fred III's wife, Lisa, who had been among the mourners, went into labor.

Less than forty-eight hours after William Trump was born, he began having seizures. In the months ahead, he would stop breathing twice. The medical bills that followed ran to nearly a third of a million dollars. Soon after the medical problems arose, Donald's younger brother, Robert, called his nephew and said not to worry, all the medical bills would be covered. For decades, Fred Trump Sr. had provided every family member with medical insurance through his company, Apartment Management Associates.

A letter from a Trump family lawyer instructed Precise, the Trump family medical plan that was part of the Trump business empire, to cover "all costs related to baby William's care, not withstanding any plan limits (percentage, number of visits, or maximum dollar amount) . . . whether or not they are deemed by Precise to be medically necessary . . . This directive shall remain in effect until further notice." The instruction was dated July 19, 1999, just twenty-four days after Fred Sr. died.

Soon after that, Fred Sr.'s will was filed in probate court. Infant William's father and the other descendants of Fred Jr. discovered that they were not collecting their anticipated share of the estate.

News reports valued Fred Sr.'s estate at somewhere between $100 million and $300 million. Its real value was no doubt more. Wealthy people contemplating the end of their lives routinely organize ownership of their assets so that tax authorities will accept values far below market rates. Generally, this is achieved by complicating the ownership structure, supposedly making it hard for individual inheritors to cash out. That can lower estate values for tax purposes by two-thirds.

Fred Trump Sr. had executed a will in 1984 after Fred Jr., his eldest son, died. That will left the bulk of his fortune to his other four children, Donald, Maryanne, Robert, and Elizabeth. His final will, which was executed in 1991—well before Fred Sr. was diagnosed with Alzheimer's in 1993—also split most of the money among those four. Little if any of the late Fred Jr.'s presumptive fifth of the fortune was left to his line; Fred III and his sister Mary (who was named for Fred Sr.'s wife) received only $200,000, the same amount given to all the other grandchildren.

Fred Sr.'s lawyer had drawn attention to the potential for litigation over the estate if the namesake son's line was cut out of the bulk of the Trump fortune. "Given the size of your estate," he wrote, leaving Fred Jr.'s children such a relatively small sum "is tantamount to disinheriting them. You may wish to increase their participation in your estate to avoid ill will in the future." The lawyer asked Fred Sr. to fill out a routine estate planning form that described his intentions. It included two boxes indicating whether he wanted to leave more money to Fred Jr.'s children, Fred III and Mary. Fred Sr. did not check those boxes.

When Fred III, Mary, and their mother, Linda, learned about the will, they filed a lawsuit—confirming the lawyer's anticipation of trouble. The lawsuit asserted that Fred Sr. was not of sound mind and that his signature on the will dated September 18, 1991, had been "procured by fraud and undue influence" by Donald and the other surviving siblings. It asked that Fred Jr.'s descendants inherit a fifth of the fortune.

Donald Trump's reaction was swift and vengeful. On March 30, 2000, one week after the lawsuit was filed, Fred III received a certified letter stating that all medical benefits would cease on May 1. For little William, that was a potential death sentence.

Lisa Trump told Heidi Evans of the *New York Daily News* that she "burst out into tears" on learning her sickly son was in jeopardy. The devastated parents filed a new lawsuit. They went to court not in Queens—where the Trump family's influence was substantial—but in Nassau County on Long Island. A judge signed an order directing that the medical coverage continue until the matter could be resolved.

Fred III said, "You have to be tough in this family. I guess I had what my father [Fred Jr.] didn't have. I will stick to my guns. I think it was just wrong." He also observed of his paternal aunts and uncles: "These are not warm and fuzzy people. They never even came to see William in the hospital. Our family puts the 'fun' in dysfunctional."

Mary said that the issue was money, of course, which was central to Fred Sr. and his four surviving children. "Given this family, it would be utterly naïve to say it has nothing to do with money," she said. "But for both me and my brother, it has much more to do with that our father [Fred Jr.] be recognized. He existed, he lived, he was their oldest son. And William is my father's grandson. He is as much a part of that family as anybody else. He desperately needs extra care."

Also speaking with Evans at the *New York Daily News*, Mary Trump said, "My aunts and uncles should be ashamed of themselves. I'm sure they are not."

Evans asked Donald Trump about this. He said that when he learned of the lawsuit over the will, his reaction was, "Why should we give him medical coverage?"

Pressed about whether it could appear coldhearted to withdraw the medical insurance of a sickly child, Trump did not waver. "I can't help that. It's cold when someone sues my father," he replied. He then added a revealing comment about the position of power that he was in compared to his nephew and his desperately ill grandnephew. Referring to Fred III, Donald said, "Had he come to see me, things could very possibly have been much different for them. . . . It's sort of disappointing. They sued my father, essentially. I'm not thrilled when someone sues my father."

Donald said he was doing nothing but carrying out the wishes of his father. "I have helped Fred [III] over the years," he said. "That was the will of my father. He had four children left, and that's who he wanted to leave his estate to."

Trump said nothing about whether he or his siblings might have had any familial or moral obligation to advise his nephew of Fred Sr.'s plans, especially since he stood to add millions to his own inheritance if the fortune was cut into fourths rather than fifths.

Maryanne Trump Barry weighed in, too. She said that Fred Jr.'s children, Mary and Fred III, were "absentee grandchildren" whom the grandparents saw only on holidays.

Donald, testifying under oath in the lawsuit challenging Fred Sr.'s will, made it clear he thought that Fred Jr.'s children had benefitted more than enough from the family fortune. "They live like kings and queens," he said under oath. "This is not two people left out in the gutter."

Years later, while seeking the Republican presidential nomination, Trump was asked about the estate tax dispute and the withdrawal of medical coverage for little William. Trump was unapologetic, a stance consistent with his statements that he has never had a reason to seek God's forgiveness and never has. "Why do I have to repent or seek God's forgiveness if I am not making mistakes?" Trump asked an Iowa audience of evangelicals in 2015. The report on this in the *Christian Post* quoted his words, then referred to Trump's "alleged Christian faith."

Trump said his pique at the challenge to his father's will motivated the termination of all medical benefits for the sick child. "I was angry because they sued," he told journalist Jason Horowitz.

Fred Jr.'s line was cut out of the will, Donald said, not because he and the surviving siblings had exercised any influence over their father, but because Fred Sr. had a "tremendous dislike" for the flight attendant his son had married. In that, Fred Sr. would have been channeling his own paternal grand-mother, who disapproved of his father Friedrich's choice of the German-born Elizabeth Christ as his wife.

Trump went on to say that the cases were settled "very am-icably." Neither Fred III nor his mother would comment when asked about Donald's remarks—which would be consistent with a settlement requiring no public disclosure by any of the parties. The "very amicable" terms remain unknown because the settlement was sealed. What provisions, if any, were made for the lifelong care of William, whose seizures eventually de-veloped into cerebral palsy, are also unknown.

Donald Trump's application of his motto of vengeance on his blood relatives, a motto directly contrary to the most basic teaching of all Christian faiths, caused deep division within his family. In contrast to this, he had years earlier developed a close relationship with one of the most vicious and heartless men who ever lived in America, a mentor who also believed revenge was the best policy and who became a kind of second father: the notorious Roy Cohn.

5

—

MAKING FRIENDS

n 1970—two years after getting his college degree from
Penn—Donald Trump was still living in Queens. He was an
outer-borough guy, part of the group derided as "bridge and
tunnel people" by the stylish Manhattanites. Trump wanted
to join and eventually lead that fashionable tribe.

Trump has boasted often that he was on the hunt "almost
every night" for "beautiful young women," but he was also
trying to make other significant connections. One of the first
and most important connections was with the notorious attorney Roy Cohn. Cohn had been the chief lawyer for Senator
Joseph McCarthy, whose communist witch hunts only ended
when he went after the United States Army.

By Trump's account, Cohn became a business mentor and
nearly a second father to him. Their steadily deepening relationship would link Trump to mob-owned construction companies at a time when other builders were begging the FBI to
crack down on the Mafia. It also ensnared Trump in a jewelry

tax scam and in a lawsuit that blew up in his face. In Cohn, Trump had someone who could be "vicious" on his behalf and who he said, looking back in 2005, "would brutalize for you."

While the timeline is fuzzy, Trump says that to become part of the Manhattan crowd he rented what he called a crummy little apartment with a view of a water tank at Third Avenue and 75th Street on the East Side. Then he set out to join Le Club, which Trump regarded as "the hottest club in the city and perhaps the most exclusive—like Studio 54 at its height. Its membership included some of the most successful men and most beautiful women in the world. It was the sort of place where you were likely to see a wealthy seventy-five-year-old guy walk in with three blondes from Sweden."

At Le Club, Trump met and studied a lot of rich men from New York and abroad, including Cohn, whom he had known by reputation.

"I don't kid myself about Roy," Trump wrote. "He was no Boy Scout. He once told me he'd spent more than two thirds of his adult life under indictment on one charge or another." Such a revelation might repulse some people, but Trump's reaction was: "That amazed me."

Trump first hired Cohn to sue the federal government. In the summer of 1972, the federal government investigated claims of racial bias involving a number of apartment house operators, including the Trumps, who owned 14,000 apartments in Brooklyn. It was not the first allegation of Trump bias. Fred Trump had faced similar accusations two decades earlier, both from the government and from legendary folk singer Woody Guthrie.

Guthrie had moved into an apartment at Beach Haven, Fred Trump's first major housing project, in 1950, soon after the six-building, 1,800-unit apartment project was completed.

Guthrie noticed that everyone around him was white, and started writing about the rental policies at what he called "bitch havens":

> I suppose that Old Man Trump knows just how
>   much racial hate
> He stirred up in that bloodpot of human hearts
> When he drawed that color line
> Here at his Beach Haven family project.

Guthrie is best known for "This Land Is Your Land," his ballad about the Dust Bowl, which gave farmers in his native Oklahoma an extra kick in the pants during the Great Depression. He set his thoughts about Trump's rental policies to a song he titled "Old Man Trump." The lyrics continue with this:

> Beach Haven ain't my home!
> No, I just can't pay this rent!
> My money's down the drain,
> And my soul is badly bent!
> Beach Haven is Trump's Tower
> Where no black folks come to roam,
> No, no, Old Man Trump!
> Old Beach Haven ain't my home!

More than two decades later, in July 1972, the federal government authorized a series of field tests for compliance with the 1968 Fair Housing Act, which Congress had passed into law one week after the assassination of Martin Luther King Jr. In these tests, a black woman or man or couple was sent to ask about renting an apartment. When they were told none were available, whites with the same information about their employment and income showed up. At Trump's Shore Haven apartments, the superintendent told a white woman she could have her pick of two units shortly after a black woman had been told there were no vacancies.

The Trumps did rent to African Americans, Puerto Ricans, and others not considered white, but only in certain buildings that were heavily minority, government investigators said. Court records showed that minority applicants were routinely steered to these other properties.

The Justice Department sued Donald Trump, his father, and Trump Management "for refusing to rent dwellings and negotiate the rental of dwellings with persons because of race and color." The case, filed in October 1973, was one of the highest profile racial discrimination cases of the many filed in federal courthouses in the wake of the Fair Housing Act.

Most big landlords settled quickly to avoid nasty publicity, agreeing to keep track of the racial mix of tenants, to advertise to non-whites, and to take other steps to comply with federal law. But Donald Trump sought advice from Cohn in what he says was their first conversation (even though Trump has testified under oath that he met Cohn three years earlier).

Trump wrote that he told Cohn, "I don't like lawyers," because they delay deals, say no, and "are always looking to settle instead of fight." Cohn surprised him by expressing agreement. Asked for his advice on what to do about the discrimination lawsuit, which Trump says an unnamed Wall Street law firm had advised settling, Cohn said, "Tell them to go to hell and fight the thing in court and let them prove that you discriminated," adding that Trump had no obligation to "rent to tenants who would be undesirable, white or black." Cohn also counseled that the accusation of racist practices would stick with Trump, so the young real estate mogul needed to defend his name.

Two months after this supposed first conversation with Cohn, Trump held a press conference at the New York Hilton, where he accused the Justice Department of fabricating a case just to force him and his father to rent to people on welfare, even though the case was about racial discrimination, not welfare. Cohn filed a lawsuit demanding $100 million in damages from the federal government. This marked a key moment in Trump's career, adopting the tactic that would be a core tenet of his 2016 presidential bid: hitting back harder when he feels attacked.

The government's lawsuit and Trump's countersuit were heard in federal court in Brooklyn a few weeks later. Cohn squared off against a twenty-six-year-old government lawyer on her first big case, an uneven match of experience that should have benefitted the Trump side. In a sworn statement, Trump asserted that neither he nor his company "to the best of my knowledge discriminated or [has] shown bias in renting our apartments." The judge was savvy enough to note the key phrase in the affidavit, which was Trump's knowledge, not any actual discrimination by the company and its employees.

Cohn argued that a government census of Trump's tenants was unnecessary, because the Trumps had seen black people in several of their buildings. He added that he had personally driven by and seen black people walking into or out of "some" Trump buildings without specifying whether these were the buildings where the lawsuit said blacks were steered or the ones the government said were kept all white.

Other facts pointed to Trump's wrongdoing. The government had been told by Trump employees that when blacks insisted on filling out an application at one of the whites-only Trump buildings, the applications were coded with "No. 9" or "C." Elyse Goldweber, the novice Justice Department lawyer, told the court that one employee who spoke to investigators was not being named because "he was afraid that the Trumps would have him 'knocked off,' or words to that effect" for revealing the techniques used to deny blacks and other minorities. Cohn's response was to accuse another government lawyer of soliciting false testimony and conducting "Gestapo-like interrogation" of Trump employees.

Federal judge Edward R. Neaher dismissed as "utterly without foundation" Cohn's claims of official misconduct. Judge Neaher also dismissed Trump's countersuit and allowed the government to proceed with the original suit and investigation, satisfied that enough evidence existed for that case to go forward.

In *The Art of the Deal*, Trump said he told Cohn, "I'd rather fight than fold, because as soon as you fold once you get the reputation" of someone who settles cases. But faced with a case in which neither facts nor the law were on his side, Trump folded and settled. A government press release heralded the settlement as "one of the most far reaching ever" to end racial discrimination in housing. The settlement required the running of advertisements to solicit non-white tenants and an end to all discriminatory practices—including the secret coding of rental applications.

Trump handled the adverse settlement the way he had learned from his father: by spinning the news and offering a simple and quotable narrative, exploiting the fact that most reporters accurately quote what people say without understanding legal rules or regulatory practice. The settlement was a complete loss for Trump, but he spun the case as a massive win, writing, "In the end the government couldn't prove its case, and we ended up making a minor settlement without admitting any guilt." The government routinely lets people who settle get off without admitting to any wrongdoing, so long as they agree to stop what they don't have to admit they were up to.

Trump's takeaway from this early loss was not that times had changed and civil rights laws would be enforced. He wrote that he learned to make sure Cohn, and presumably other lawyers who followed, was fully prepared when a case went to court. He also learned to place loyalty above all else.

Even if he privately disagreed, or if pursuing a case was not in Cohn's best interest, "you could count on him to go to bat for you," Trump wrote. Loyalty, he continued, was far more important than "all the hundreds of 'respectable' guys who make careers out of boasting about their uncompromising integrity but have absolutely no loyalty." That is, of course, the kind of perspective we expect from mobsters, dictators, and others whose primary regard is for unflinching support, not for allegiance to truth or facts.

The settlement required two years of federal oversight. No significant problems arose, so oversight ended. In the third year, the government filed a new complaint, asserting that discrimination in rentals resumed when oversight ended.

In a few years, Trump would learn that Cohn came with another benefit. Hiring him could ensure that his Manhattan construction projects moved smoothly. Among Cohn's other clients were two of America's most powerful Mafia figures who controlled key unions attached to demolition and construction in New York City.

6

—

TRUMP'S MOST IMPORTANT DEALS

In *The Art of the Deal*, Trump boasts that when he applied for a casino owner's license in 1981, he persuaded the New Jersey attorney general to limit the investigation of his background. It was perhaps the most lucrative negotiation of Trump's life, one that would embarrass state officials a decade later when Trump's involvement with mobsters, mob associates, and swindlers became clearer.

New Jersey required all license applicants to complete a highly detailed personal history under a system designed to fulfill the promise to New Jersey voters that Atlantic City would not become a mob-run Las Vegas East. Applicants had to fill out about fifty pages of details, including every address where they had lived in the past decade, any insurance claims of more than $100,000, extensive details on their business dealings, and any government investigations, civil or criminal. The state was so diligent in vetting would-be casino owners that it sent detectives overseas to interview people and inspect documents.

Trump was told in advance that investigations took about eighteen months. Unwilling to endure such a lengthy inquiry, Trump set about arranging special terms to prevent scrutiny of his past, a practice he has continued to this day.

First, instead of going to state government offices in Trenton, Trump asked John Degnan, the New Jersey attorney general, to come to him. Degnan and G. Michael Brown, the head of the Division of Gaming Enforcement, traveled to the Short Hills office of Nick Ribis, a New Jersey lawyer Trump had hired at the recommendation of billionaire publisher Si Newhouse.

Trump assured Degnan there was no need for a long inquiry into his conduct and business dealings; he was "clean as a whistle"—too young at age thirty-five to have become enmeshed in any sort of trouble. Trump then told him that unless the attorney general expedited approval, he would not build in Atlantic City, where he had already acquired a prime piece of land at the center of the Boardwalk. Finally, Trump hinted that his Grand Hyatt Hotel, next to Grand Central Terminal in midtown Manhattan, could accommodate its own casino. Given Trump's well-known success in convincing the City of New York to perform lucrative favors, that was a subtle but powerful threat. If New York State lawmakers authorized casinos in the Empire State, it would draw a disastrous amount of business away from Atlantic City, more than 125 miles south of Manhattan.

Degnan was about to make his own run for New Jersey governor. He knew that a Trump lawsuit, a Trump campaign for casinos in New York, or denunciations from Trump about excessive government regulation would not win him any votes. He agreed to Trump's terms. He did not promise approval, but did promise that, if Trump cooperated, the investigation would be over within six months. Trump paid Degnan back by becoming a vocal opponent of gambling anywhere in the East except Atlantic City. Nonetheless, Degnan lost his gubernatorial bid.

Of course, Trump was not clean as a whistle by the standards of the New Jersey Casino Control Commission, even though he has still never been indicted, much less convicted of any crime.

The casino license application asked whether Trump had "ever been the subject of an investigation" by a government agency "for any reason." He had, but the DGE report made no mention of two such cases and dealt with two others in a footnote, making it clear that Trump did not include them when he submitted his application.

The first investigation was a 1979 federal grand jury inquiry into how he had obtained an option to buy the Penn Central railroad yards on the West Side of Manhattan. FBI agents interviewed Trump twice, telling him the second time that he was a target of the grand jury. The tip that launched the investigation by Ed Korman—then the United States attorney in Brooklyn—came just before the five year statute of limitations was to run out. Korman's probe was not complete when the deadline came. No charges were filed.

In 1980, John Martin—the United States Attorney in Manhattan—briefly investigated Trump's deal to acquire the old Commodore Hotel, which was remade into the Grand Hyatt in Midtown Manhattan. The issue, again, involved the Penn Central yards, which (together with the Commodore) were owned by the bankrupt residue of the old Penn Central Transportation Company. At stake was whether the Commodore deal cheated the debtors in the bankruptcy case. No charges were filed.

A third omission was the FBI's questioning Trump about his dealings with John Cody, the mob associate with three felony convictions and five other arrests who, as local head of the teamsters union, controlled the flow of ready-mix concrete in New York City. Law enforcement reports described Cody as a very close associate of the Gambino crime family. Cody had a history of getting free apartments from builders who wanted to avoid trouble from labor unions. Agents had heard that Cody sought a freebie apartment from Trump. Trump denied it. No charges were filed.

The fourth case was the Justice Department's 1973 suit accusing Trump of racial discrimination in the rental of Trump apartments, prompting the unsuccessful countersuit filed by lawyer Roy Cohn. Casino owner applicants were asked about being accused of any civil misconduct, which would include racial discrimination in housing. Trump checked the "no" box.

Trump had to know that failing to reveal these matters would make him ineligible to own a casino if investigators found out he had not been candid. The cover of the application declared in large capital letters:

FAILURE TO ANSWER ANY QUESTION COMPLETELY AND TRUTHFULLY WILL RESULT IN DENIAL OF YOUR LICENSE APPLICATION.

This standard had been strictly enforced for other people. The prevailing legal case, which established how firmly the standard could be applied, involved an early applicant for a blackjack dealer's license, one of the lowest-level licenses. The woman was rejected as morally unfit. Her offense? As a teenage cashier, she had admitted to a misdemeanor for giving friends discounts, an offense she left off her dealer's license application.

After completing its investigation of Trump in a record five months, the Division of Gaming Enforcement report gave the ruling body, the Casino Control Commission, no hint that Trump had been the focus of multiple federal criminal investigations. Two of these cases had been in the newspapers. The reporter who broke the story, Wayne Barrett, was questioned by the DGE as part of the application investigation. Why the final report omitted these facts is a mystery.

The DGE gave Trump a pass on his failure to disclose. In a footnote to its 119-page report, the DGE said that just before completing its work, Trump had "volunteered" the information he had failed to disclose. It was an early sign of what two Casino Control commissioners would later say was a pattern of DGE favoritism to Trump.

But there was much more that the commissioners, who had to vote on each licensee, didn't know.

Beginning three years earlier, in 1978, Trump had hired mobbed-up construction firms to erect Trump Tower. Instead of building a high-rise skeleton of steel girders, Trump chose ready-mix concrete. He did so at a time when other New York developers, notably the LeFrak and Resnik families, were pleading with the FBI to free them from a mob-run concrete cartel that jacked up prices.

Ready-mix was a curious choice at the time. The liquid stone had to be rushed to construction sites and poured quickly to avoid costly problems like hardening in its rotating steel drums or not being wet enough to retain strength as it dried. Using ready-mix made developers vulnerable to union work stoppages, as Trump would later acknowledge. The teamsters controlled the trucks delivering the ready-mix. The construction unions controlled the construction site gate. The concrete workers and carpenters controlled the pouring and making of forms. At the top, the mob controlled the unions and rigged their elections, as a federal labor racketeering trial brought by federal prosecutor Rudy Giuliani later proved.

Trump favored concrete. The material has its advantages, like avoiding the costly fireproofing required for steel girders. Trump used ready-mix not just for the fifty-eight-story Trump Tower, but also his thirty-nine-story Trump Plaza apartment building on East 61st Street, his Trump Plaza casino hotel in Atlantic City, and other buildings.

Trump bought his Manhattan ready-mix from a company called S & A Concrete. Mafia chieftains Anthony "Fat Tony" Salerno and Paul Castellano secretly owned the firm. S & A charged the inflated prices that the LeFrak and Resnik families complained about, LeFrak to both law enforcement and *The New York Times*.

As Barrett noted, by choosing to build with ready-mix concrete rather than other materials, Trump put himself "at the mercy of a legion of concrete racketeers." But having an ally in Roy Cohn mitigated Trump's concerns. With Cohn as his fixer, Trump had no worries that the Mafia bosses would have the unions stop work on Trump Tower; Salerno and Castellano were Cohn's clients. Indeed, when the cement workers struck in summer 1982, the concrete continued to flow at Trump Tower.

Years later, Barrett—the first reporter to seriously examine Trump's business practices—was able to expose some of Trump's dealings. Barrett enjoyed the deep trust of numerous local, state, and federal law enforcement sources. He reported that two witnesses observed Trump meeting at Cohn's town house with Salerno, an association that itself could have cost Trump his casino owner's license. When the Salerno meeting became public knowledge, the DGE did not seek out the witnesses, who, though unnamed, any detective could have identified easily. Or, if it did, its report gave no hint of such an inquiry. Instead, the DGE put Trump under oath. He denied meeting Salerno. Case closed.

Just as revealing was Trump's association with John Cody, the corrupt head of Teamsters Local 282. Cody, under indictment when he ordered the citywide strike in 1982, directed that concrete deliveries continue to Trump Tower. Cody told Barrett, "Donald liked to deal with me through Roy Cohn."

Cody's son, Michael, told me that his father was both a loving dad and every bit the notorious racketeer people believed him to be. He said that, as a boy, he listened in when Trump called his father, imploring Cody to make sure concrete flowed steadily at Trump Tower so he would not go broke before it was finished.

While Cody did not get a Trump Tower apartment, as the FBI suspected, an especially gorgeous woman friend did. She had no known job and attributed her lavish lifestyle to the kindness of friends. She bought three Trump Tower apartments directly under the triplex where Donald and his then wife, Ivana, lived. John Cody invested $100,000 in the woman's apartments and stayed there often. Trump helped the woman get a $3 million mortgage to pay for the three apartments, one of which she modified to include the only indoor swimming pool in Trump Tower. She said she got the mortgage from a bank that Trump recommended she use, without filling out a loan application or showing financials.

After Cody was convicted of racketeering, imprisoned, and no longer in control of the union, Trump sued the woman for $250,000 for alteration work. She countersued for $20 million. Her court papers accused Trump of taking kickbacks from contractors. They further asserted that this could "be the basis of a criminal proceeding" against Trump if the state attorney general were to investigate.

Trump, who insists in his presidential campaign that he never settles lawsuits because that just encourages more of them, quickly settled. He paid the woman $500,000. He has testified that he hardly knew those involved, and that there was nothing improper in his dealings with either the woman or John Cody.

Federal prosecutors soon brought a major case against eight mobsters. The charges included inflating the price of concrete for Trump's East 61st Street apartment building. In 1986, Salerno and seven others, including the head of the concrete workers union, were convicted in a racketeering trial that included murder, payoffs, and inflated prices for concrete. The chief trial prosecutor, Michael Chertoff, told the judge that the defendants were "directing the largest and most vicious criminal business in the history of the United States."

Even after he got his casino license, Trump continued to have relationships that should have prompted inquiries by the casino investigators.

In 1988, Trump made a deal to put his name on Trump Golden Series and Trump Executive Series limousines, as reporter Bill Bastone first revealed. In addition to a TV with a videocassette player and a fax machine, each limo had two telephones. Stemware and a handy liquor dispenser were nestled in rosewood cabinets. A hood ornament melded the Trump and Cadillac brands. The limos were modified at the Dillinger Coach Works, which was owned by a pair of convicted felons.

The first was convicted extortionist Jack Schwartz; the other was convicted thief John Staluppi, a multimillionaire Long Island car dealer identified in FBI reports and other law enforcement documents as a soldier in the Colombo crime family. New Jersey casino regulators (who claimed to oversee the most highly regulated industry in American history) did nothing when Trump made his deal with Staluppi and Schwartz to sell the Trump-branded Cadillacs.

New York liquor regulators proved to be much tougher. They denied Staluppi's application for a liquor license because of his rap sheet and his extensive dealings with mobsters, including some common friends who provided Trump with his helicopters, as we shall see. But first, a look at Trump's football team.

7

—

"A GREAT LAWSUIT"

Erecting gaudy buildings did not bring Donald Trump the national attention he craved. It was football that made him famous. Hiring a new general manager for his real estate firm drew little media attention, but "I hire a coach for a football team and there are sixty or seventy reporters calling to interview me."

Trump's foray into professional football provides an early example of a business career built on breaking, ignoring, or making up rules.

In August 1983, Trump bought the New Jersey Generals, one of a dozen teams in the nascent United States Football League. The league played its first game in March 1983, five weeks after Super Bowl XVI. The USFL drew decent crowds, but nothing like the National Football League, which took in about $1 billion at the gate that year and another $2.1 billion from network television broadcasts.

Back then, NFL teams were valued in the tens of millions of dollars. Serial sports entrepreneur David Dixon and other USFL founders had started the league as a way for people not rich enough to buy an NFL team (like Trump) to invest in commercial sports. Trump initially said he paid $9 million for the Generals; he later claimed $5 million (which annoyed the other owners by implicitly reducing the value of their investments).

Dixon's strategy was low-risk and low-cost. It called for patience and careful execution to grow the business until it could go head-to-head with the NFL. A crucial part of that strategy was to play in the spring rather than compete with the NFL's wealth, seven decades of fans, and monopoly in the fall season.

USFL attendance averaged about twenty-five thousand per game, a respectable number for a new league. Both the ABC network and a television start-up called ESPN signed contracts to broadcast USFL games. That brought in additional cash to supplement the ticket sales and other direct fan revenue that would eventually turn losses into profits if the business strategy was executed smartly.

The new league embraced innovations that fans liked, some of which the stodgy NFL later adopted. For example, when USFL players scored touchdowns they could dance, holler, and otherwise celebrate, in clear contrast to NFL rules that prohibited such conduct at the time. The new league also saw the benefits of videotape. Years earlier, the NFL had considered instant replays so fans could make their own assessments of controversial decisions by the referees, but rejected the idea. The USFL adopted instant replay, which fans embraced. It is now, of course, a staple in broadcasting all professional sports.

Trump had little interest in Dixon's strategy. Instead, he endowed the USFL with the showmanship and high-stakes gambling that would ultimately destroy it. Applying his P. T.

Barnum–like skills at attracting attention, Trump held cheer-leader tryouts in the basement of Trump Tower just before Christmas 1983. A flock of television cameras showed up to record the more than four hundred high-kicking candidates jostling to become "Brig-A-Dears," as the Generals' cheerlead-ers were called. Trump's eclectic choice of judges also ensured news coverage. Among them were *New York Post* gossip col-umnist Cindy Adams, pop artists LeRoy Neiman and Andy Warhol, as well as Ivana Trump, who designed the cleavage-maximizing Brig-A-Dear outfits.

To promote the team, Trump sent the Brig-A-Dears to bars. He did not spend money on security to deal with the inevita-ble boors and drunks who mistook the scantily clad young women for hookers. Though she was underage and could not participate herself, sixteen-year-old Brig-A-Dear Lisa Edel-stein organized a walkout by the adult cheerleaders to pro-test the lack of protection at "sleazy bars." In a 2015 interview, Edelstein (who has starred on the television shows *House* and *Girlfriends' Guide to Divorce*) said that although she had later dealings with him, "Trump doesn't remember this" walkout.

Signing top college players and luring several pros away from the NFL also helped the Generals build an audience. De-spite the league salary cap of less than $2 million, Trump hired a star athlete, notably Heisman Trophy–winning quarterback Doug Flutie from Boston College, for well over the maximum USFL salary. None of this was consistent with Dixon's low-risk, low-cost plan to slowly and steadily build the business.

After his first season as team owner ended, Trump decided to go for the NFL's jugular—a commercial infant taking on a successful and powerful adult in its prime. In 1984, Trump persuaded the other USFL owners to sue the NFL under the Sherman Antitrust Act, which makes it a felony to "monopolize, or attempt to monopolize" any business. The suit was filed in October. It said the NFL should not have had contracts with more than two of the three television networks. Trump's theory was that, since the NFL had television contracts with all three networks, the USFL could not get its games on the air if it switched to a fall season, so the NFL must have had an unlawful monopoly on fall football. "If God wanted football in the spring," he told an ABC television reporter, "he wouldn't have created baseball."

Antitrust litigation is a legal specialty as arcane as tax law. Mastering antitrust law requires years of experience and a grounding in the subtle economics of anti-competitive behavior, as well as a thorough understanding of past court decisions. Such a suit would require a top antitrust litigator with a record of success with juries. This was not to be.

The lawsuit was signed by Trump's mentor and attack dog, Roy Cohn. As the two men announced the lawsuit on October 18, 1984, Cohn said he had a list of NFL owners on a secret committee "created exclusively for the purpose of combatting the USFL." Reporters asked for proof. "We have reliable reason to believe we know who they are and what they are doing," Cohn replied. When reporters persisted, Cohn channeled his patron, Senator Joseph McCarthy, who would wave a paper on which he claimed to have the names of communist agents in high-level positions in the federal government, but whom he never identified. Like McCarthy, Cohn declined to name names.

For the trial, Trump convinced the other USFL team owners to hire Harvey D. Myerson, a colorful litigator with no expertise in antitrust litigation. The federal court trial lasted forty-eight days, filled with mind-numbing testimony about law and economics, as well as testimony from Trump himself, claiming NFL commissioner Pete Rozelle had tried to buy him off—an accusation that could well be an indictable offense. A judge handling the case seemed unimpressed with this, writing without further comment that Trump "testified that he was offered an NFL franchise by Commissioner Rozelle in exchange for his blocking the USFL's proposed move to the fall and his preventing the league from filing the instant action. Rozelle denied that he made such an offer to Trump."

After five days of deliberation, the jury found that the NFL had indeed engaged in criminal behavior when, as an appeals court later put it, the league "willfully acquired or maintained monopoly power in a market consisting of major-league professional football in the United States." They awarded the USFL damages in the amount of one dollar.

Under the Sherman Antirust Act, the award was automatically tripled to three dollars.

The tiny damages sent a powerful message, which many at the time interpreted as both acknowledgment of the illegal monopoly and recognition that the USFL should not have taken up two months of the jurors' lives by seeking quick-and-easy riches from a lawsuit.

Years later, after the Supreme Court declined to hear the matter, the NFL sent a check to the USFL, adding to the three dollars the legally required interest: seventy-six cents. The uncashed check remains stored in USFL executive director Steve Ehrhart's Memphis safe-deposit box, no doubt worth more as sports memorabilia than its face value.

Trump's legal strategy had failed. The networks wouldn't have to worry about broadcasting a fall USFL season. On top of that, they were annoyed by the lawsuit. They were not defendants themselves, but they were so integral to the scheme the jury examined that they were forced to spend money protecting their own interests. Within minutes of the jury's verdict, USFL team owners were telling reporters it was over. The USFL promptly folded, and what could have been a successful long-term enterprise turned to dust; the smart business strategy of David Dixon had been fumbled by a disastrous Trumpian legal gamble. Myerson (who later spent seventy months in prison for tax evasion and years of overbilling in what prosecutors called "a one-man crime wave") was mystified by the verdict and promised an appeal.

In 1988, the Second Circuit Court of Appeals explicitly rejected the theory Trump had sold to the other owners—that a lawsuit was an appropriate way to force the NFL to merge with the USFL. The court, in the formal language of legal opinions, chastised both Trump and the owners who went along with him. Judge Ralph K. Winter Jr. wrote that "what the USFL seeks is essentially a judicial restructuring of major-league professional football to allow it to enter" into a merger with the NFL.

Calling the NFL "a highly successful entertainment product," Judge Winter observed that "new sports leagues must be prepared to make the investment of time, effort and money that develops interest and fan loyalty and results in an attractive product for the media. The jury in the present case obviously found that patient development of a loyal following among fans and an adherence to an original plan that offered long-run gains were lacking . . . The jury found that the failure of the USFL was not the result of the NFL's television contracts but of its own decision to seek entry into the NFL on the cheap."

The appeals court decision, which the United States Supreme Court let stand, was a stinging rebuke of Trump's effort to use litigation to obtain what he was unwilling to achieve by patiently devoting time, money, and effort in the market.

Years later, Trump would appear in an ESPN documentary by Mike Tollin called *Small Potatoes: Who Killed the USFL?* The title came from Trump's own response when Tollin suggested that the USFL could have survived had it stuck to a spring season format.

The documentary includes a shot from the USFL days showing a smiling Trump looking into the camera and expressing his support for Tollin, along with his expectation that Tollin would not be well-rounded in his filmmaking, but biased in favor of Trump. "Mike will only use the good," says Trump. "Mike's a star maker."

At the time, Tollin ran the company that filmed USFL games and stitched together highlights, which he considered a dream job. When Tollin interviewed Trump a quarter century later for his ESPN documentary, Trump grew annoyed by questions about whether the lawsuit was the smart strategy and whether a spring football league could have prospered. "It would have been small potatoes," Trump says as he pulls off his microphone and walks out. The documentary also includes Trump summarizing his thoughts years after the USFL fold: "It was a nice experience," he says. "It was fun. We had a great lawsuit."

Tollin extended Trump a courtesy in 2009 by sending him a rough cut of the film before it aired on ESPN. Trump was not happy with what he saw. In what had long before become a pattern when he was displeased, Trump took a thick, felt-tip pen to Tollin's letter before mailing it back: "A third rate documentary and extremely dishonest—as you know. Best wishes," Trump wrote, adding his distinctive, jaws-like signature. "P.S.—You are a loser." Trump underlined the last word.

To disagree with Trump is to be wrong. To portray Trump in a way that does not fit with his image of himself is to be a loser. It is an approach to life that may work in business (where Trump can walk out and not deal with people who displease him), but government leaders do not enjoy that luxury, especially the president of the United States.

If the Senate and House leadership do not do as the president wishes, he cannot dismiss them. The Constitution makes Congress coequal. The same is true of the Supreme Court. Leaders of sovereign nations—whether democratically elected politicians as in Canada, Europe, and Mexico, heirs to the throne as in much of the Middle East, or self-appointed autocrats as in China, Cuba, and North Korea—also cannot be dismissed in the way Trump walked out on Tollin and others who have not embraced his self-image over the years. Everyone cannot be expected to "use only the good."

The ruinous legal strategy Trump sold to the other USFL team owners was not the only time that he would flout conventional rules of conduct. After the USFL failed, Trump drafted a letter on Trump Organization stationery. This letter sought leniency for a major cocaine and marijuana trafficker with multiple connections to Trump, a man whose case would soon come before a federal judge in New Jersey—a judge who just happened to be Trump's older sister, who recused herself from the case three weeks later.

8

—

SHOWING MERCY

Among the assorted criminals with whom Trump did
business over more than three decades, his most mysterious dealings involved a drug trafficker named Joseph
Weichselbaum. Trump did unusual favors for the three-
time felon, repeatedly putting his lucrative casino license at
risk to help a major cocaine and marijuana trafficker for reasons that remain unfathomable.

The Brooklyn-born Weichselbaum, four years older than
Trump, was well-known in Miami cigarette-boat-racing circles, where narcotics traffickers and white-collar felons often
mixed. He piloted boats named *Mighty Mouse* and *Nuts 'n Bolts*
in races off the Florida coast. He came in third at a 1973 race
behind Charles F. Keating, a Cincinnati lawyer who later went
to prison in the Lincoln Savings and Loan Association swindle
that cost taxpayers $2 billion.

Trump met Joey Weichselbaum through Steve Hyde, the
portly Mormon elder who ran Trump's Atlantic City casi-

nos in 1986. At the time, Weichselbaum was already a twice-convicted felon. His first offense was grand theft auto in 1965. His second was embezzlement in 1979. A judge ordered Weichselbaum to return $135,000 to S&S Corrugated Paper Machinery, a Brooklyn firm at which he had worked for a decade.

Weichselbaum and his younger brother, Franklin (who has never been charged with a crime), launched a New Jersey–based helicopter service in 1982. Many more experienced firms offered helicopter services, but in 1984 the Weichselbaum brothers landed the primary contract to ferry high rollers to and from Trump casinos. Their fleet served other casinos as well, but their main client was Trump. The brothers' company also maintained Trump's personal helicopter, a black Eurocopter AS332 Super Puma he named *Ivana*—after his wife at the time—that Trump valued at $10 million.

And Joey Weichselbaum was not the only felon Trump selected to provide helicopter flights for high rollers. He also retained Dillinger Charter Services, whose owners included John Staluppi, identified in law enforcement reports as a member of the Gambino crime family.

The brothers Weichselbaum called their firm Damin Aviation. Joey's title was general manager. Damin Aviation was part of a convoluted financial arrangement that included Alan Turtletaub, founder of a high-interest-rate second-mortgage firm called The Money Store. A Turtletaub company bought the helicopters and then resold them to an intermediary firm, who in turn leased them to Damin Aviation. The deal required little if any cash, thanks to a combination of tax shelter financing and tax-free bonds provided by the New Jersey Economic Development Administration.

Damin soon filed for bankruptcy and reorganized as Nimad (*Damin* spelled backward). The new firm kept Trump's business, which is not unusual in itself; when a debtor retains possession of a firm, as the Weichselbaums did, the debtor often retains contracts with customers. But the firm went bankrupt again, and again reorganized, this time as American Business Aviation.

Why did Trump Plaza continue to pay $100,000 per month and Trump's Castle $80,000 a month for helicopter services from a firm that was so financially unstable when Trump could have hired any its better-financed and more experienced competitors? One obvious question is whether Weichselbaum was perhaps providing some other valuable service sub rosa.

Trump himself was no drug user. He didn't even drink or smoke. But it was open knowledge in Atlantic City that high rollers could get anything they wanted as long as it was done discreetly. For those who brought lots of cash, signed big markers, or were assigned complimentary suites, certain butlers were known to provide, for a price, whatever the customer wanted—be it illicit sex, drugs, or anything else. As a state casino lawyer told me shortly after I arrived in Atlantic City in 1988, "We regulate what goes on involving gaming, not what people do in the privacy of hotel rooms."

Another glaring question is whether Trump financed any of Weichselbaum's activities. Trump was known to be an avid investor seeking big returns, whether through greenmailing competing casino companies—buying controlling shares in rival casino companies and selling back those shares at a higher price—or using Roy Cohn's influence with mob-owned companies and mob-controlled unions.

Joey Weichselbaum's pay and perks were unusual. Even though he had officially left the twice-failed helicopter company, Weichselbaum continued to receive his $100,000 annual salary. He also retained his company car and driver. All the while, he was deeply involved in drug trafficking in Florida,

Ohio, Kentucky, and Tennessee, according to his 1985 indictment by a federal grand jury in Cincinnati. One shipment
alone involved three-quarters of a ton of marijuana.

In addition to his helicopter business, Joey Weichselbaum
was an officer at a used-car dealership north of Miami—
Bradford Motors, which he also owned in partnership with
his brother. Couriers from Colombia delivered drugs there,
which were sometimes sold on the spot. According to the indictment, Weichselbaum put cocaine in vehicles himself or
handed it over to couriers who delivered it to buyers. The
dealership, essentially a front for drug trafficking, paid phony
commissions for the sale of cars in an effort to hide the real
business, as court records show.

As a casino owner in Atlantic City, Trump had every reason
to avoid business dealings with known criminals, which Weichselbaum was even before the drug trafficking and tax evasion
charges in Cincinnati. Under the New Jersey Casino Control
Act, Trump and all casino owners were "required to establish
by clear and convincing evidence" his or her "good character,
honesty and integrity. Such information shall include, without
limitation, information pertaining to family, habits, character,
reputation, criminal and arrest record, business activities, financial affairs, and business, professional and personal associates."

Yet, instead of dropping the helicopter service, Trump
retained American Business Aviation for his casino shuttles
and to service his personal helicopter. Trump later acquired
three helicopters when he divvied up the old Resorts International casino company in a deal with entertainer Merv Griffin.
Trump got the unfinished Taj Mahal casino hotel, Merv the
aging Resorts hotel (the original Atlantic City casino). Despite
having these three choppers, Trump kept paying more than $2
million per year for Weichselbaum copters.

Two months after Weichselbaum was indicted, the Weichselbaum brothers rented apartment 32-C at the Trump Plaza condominiums on East 61st Street in Manhattan. Trump personally owned apartment 32-C. The rental terms were unusual. Rent was $7,000 per month, which was at the low end of a reasonable rate. The brothers paid $3,000 a month in cash—using checks made out to Donald J. Trump personally—and paid the rest in helicopter services. Short of a costly forensic audit, it would be impossible for any law enforcement agency, including New Jersey casino regulators, to ascertain whether the brothers actually paid any more than the cash rent. What motivated Trump to agree to this arrangement has never been explained.

When Weichselbaum made a deal with prosecutors to plead guilty to one of the eighteen counts in the Cincinnati case, something very suspicious happened. His case was transferred out of Ohio for the guilty plea and the sentencing. Logically, the case might have gone to South Florida, where Bradford Motors was located, or to New York, where Weichselbaum lived. Indeed, that is exactly what Weichselbaum's Ohio lawyer, Arnold Morelli, sought in a January 30, 1986, motion requesting his case be transferred to either Manhattan or Miami for "the convenience of human beings such as the defendant and witnesses." Instead, the Weichselbaum case was moved to New Jersey. There it was assigned to Judge Maryanne Trump Barry—Donald Trump's older sister.

Judge Barry recused herself three weeks later, as judicial ethics required, but the mere act of removing herself from the case came with a powerful message: a sitting federal judge, as well as her husband (lawyer John Barry) and family, repeatedly flew in helicopters connected to a major drug trafficker. Any new judge assigned to the case, including the district's presiding judge, was on notice that this case had the potential to embarrass the bench.

When Judge Harold A. Ackerman replaced Trump's sister, Trump wrote him a letter seeking leniency for Weichselbaum on the drug trafficking charge. Trump characterized the defendant as "a credit to the community" and described Weichselbaum as "conscientious, forthright and diligent" in his dealings with the Trump Plaza and Trump's Castle casinos. When asked about the letter under oath in a private 1990 meeting with New Jersey Division of Gaming Enforcement lawyers, Trump testified that he could not recall whether "he had written any letters of reference to the federal judge who sentenced Weichselbaum." Subsequently, the division obtained such a letter, and Trump acknowledged that it bore his signature.

Two years later, the DGE had to explain itself publicly after journalist Wayne Barrett's unauthorized 1992 biography of Trump revealed the letter. The DGE, citing my reporting on the issue, published a report on fourteen issues raised by Barrett. Its report said nothing about what would prompt Trump to write such a letter, whether he actually believed what he wrote, and what his purpose was in writing it. The DGE lawyers merely recorded Trump's denial, then later his admission that he had in fact signed the letter. That was typical of the DGE lawyers, who declined again and again to ask probing questions that might raise deeper issues about Trump's fitness to hold a license.

Likewise, the DGE's response to Barrett's book did not request an explanation of the unusual terms under which Trump rented an apartment he personally owned to the Weichselbaum brothers. As with other matters—like the accusations made by high roller Bob Libutti—the DGE took

Trump at his word and avoided asking questions that might require more investigation.

Judge Ackerman gave Weichselbaum a sentence that stood in stark contrast to the sentences levied on the others named in the Cincinnati indictment. The small fish got sentences of up to twenty years; Weichselbaum, the ringleader, got three. He served only eighteen months. When he was up for early release, Weichselbaum told his parole officer that he already had work lined up. He was Donald Trump's new helicopter consultant. He also said he would be moving into Trump Tower. While he was behind bars, Weichselbaum's girlfriend bought two adjoining thirty-ninth-story Trump Tower apartments (numbered 49-A and 49-B because Trump skipped tenth-floor numbers to inflate the apparent height of his signature building erected a few years earlier). The price was $2.4 million. Trump confirmed to the DGE that he believed Weichselbaum moved into Trump Tower and lived with a girlfriend after he was released from prison, but said he had no contact with him except for seeing him in the building.

Weichselbaum also told his probation officer that he had known about Marla Maples, Trump's mistress, long before that relationship became public knowledge. He said he tried to talk Trump into ending the affair. He said Trump asked him to let Marla stay at the Trump Plaza high-rise apartment the Weichselbaum brothers rented from him, just a few blocks from Trump Tower. The DGE dismissed this, saying simply that it was "not in possession of any credible information which would suggest that DJT asked Weichselbaum to permit his friend Marla Maples to reside in the Weichselbaum condominium. DJT has emphatically denied this allegation."

The report offered no indication that the DGE had interviewed Weichselbaum, his brother, Maples, the probation officer, or anyone else who might have contradicted Trump's denial. Again, not asking questions was key to how the DGE protected its own reputation while simultaneously protecting casino owners from themselves.

As a casino owner, Trump could have lost his license for associating with Weichselbaum. But the DGE never asked whether he had any financial entanglement, obviously undisclosed, with Weichselbaum or anyone connected to him, including whether he had staked any of the drug deals, based on its publicly released reports. Without the DGE putting into the public record the very obvious questions, together with the answers, about what motivated Trump to make such risky moves—including denying the letter he wrote seeking soft treatment for Weichselbaum—we can only speculate about what may have influenced Trump's conduct regarding the drug trafficker.

Trump called my home in spring 2016, when I was working on a long piece for *Politico* magazine about his ties to various criminals. After a few questions about what I was up to, Trump asked what I wanted to know, even though he already had my twenty-one questions in writing. I asked what motivated him to write the letter for Weichselbaum. Trump said he "hardly knew" the man and didn't remember anything about him. When I reminded Trump that he said on national television just a few months earlier that he has "the world's greatest memory," Trump just said that "that was long ago."

As Trump often does in calls to journalists, he told me he liked some of my work and that I had been fair at times. Then, with a pause, he added that if he didn't like what I was about to publish he would sue me. That last comment surprised me a bit. Trump knows that I am not intimidatable. I reminded him that he is a public figure. Under the law, that means a libel suit would require him to show that I wrote something with reckless disregard for the truth—something no one has ever accused me of in nearly fifty years of investigative reporting.

"I know I'm a public figure but I'll sue you anyway," he said before ringing off.

Weichselbaum was not the last unsavory character Trump got close to. Much more recently, Trump chose to work with a convicted art thief who goes by the name "Joey No Socks," as well as with the son of a Russian mob boss, a man with a violent history . . . and there's video to prove it.

9

—

POLISH BRIGADE

Before Donald Trump could erect Trump Tower—his signature building—on Fifth Avenue, he had to knock down the Bonwit Teller department store, which had catered to fashionable women since 1929.

Bonwit's twelve-story façade was adorned with a pair of giant bas-relief panels considered priceless examples of the Art Deco era: two naked women with flowing scarves, dancers perhaps, cut in limestone. The building's entry featured an immense grillwork made from Benedict nickel, hammered aluminum, and other materials, which gave it the impression of a lusciously large piece of jewelry when backlit at night. *American Architect* magazine's 1929 appraisal of the building described it as "a sparkling jewel in keeping with the character of the store."

Trump assured those worried about the architectural treasures that he would give them to the Metropolitan Museum of Art if removal was not prohibitively expensive, a promise he would not keep.

Instead of hiring an experienced demolition contractor, Trump chose Kaszycki & Sons Contractors, a window washing business owned by a Polish émigré. Upward of two hundred men began demolishing the building in midwinter 1980. The men worked without hard hats. They lacked facemasks, even though asbestos—known to cause incurable cancers—swirled all around them. They didn't have goggles to protect their eyes from the bits of concrete and steel that sometimes flew through the air like bullets. The men didn't have power tools either; they brought down the twelve-story building with sledgehammers.

Trump kept an eye on the project, not just when visiting the site (where photographs show him smiling under a hard hat), but from an office he rented directly across Fifth Avenue, which offered him an unobstructed view.

The demolition workers were not American citizens, but "had recently arrived from Poland," a federal court later determined. The court also found that "they were undocumented and worked 'off the books.' No payroll records were kept, no Social Security or other taxes were withheld and they were not paid in accordance with wage laws. They were told they would be paid $4.00 or in some cases $5.00 an hour for working 12-hour shifts seven days a week. In fact, they were paid irregularly and incompletely."

Many members of the demolition crew, which became known as the Polish Brigade, lived at the work site, sleeping through the bitter cold on bare concrete floors. The crew numbered about thirty or forty in the daytime, but swelled to as many as two hundred at night, when few people would be around the tony business district to observe the demolition work.

Fed up that their paychecks kept bouncing, some of the

workers corralled Thomas Macari, Trump's personal representative. They showed him to the edge of one of the higher floors and asked if he would like them to hang him over the side. The workers, likely hungry, demanded their pay. Otherwise, no work.

When Macari told his boss what had happened, Trump placed a panicked telephone call to Daniel Sullivan—a labor fixer, FBI informant, suspect in the disappearance of Jimmy Hoffa, and Trump's personal negotiator for the Grand Hyatt contract with the hotel workers' union.

"Donald told me he was having some difficulties," Sullivan later testified, "and he admitted to me that—seeking my advice—he had some illegal Polish employees on the job. I reacted by saying to Donald that 'I think you are nuts.' I told him to fire them promptly if he had any brains."

As Sullivan later told me, along with reporter Wayne Barrett and others, hiring Polish workers who were in the country illegally and then having them work without standard safety equipment was not just foolish, it was reckless. For all his dealings with Trump, Sullivan was repeatedly astonished by the businessman's lack of prudence. He said that whenever Trump saw an opportunity to collect more money or to cut his costs by not paying people what they had earned, he did. "Common sense just never took hold" when Trump had money on his mind, Sullivan told me several times.

To Sullivan, only greed and an utter lack of regard for human life could allow Trump to let the Polish Brigade work without hard hats or the facemasks they needed to keep asbestos from entering their lungs. "Men were stripping electric wires with their bare hands," Sullivan later testified.

There is no record of any federal, state, or city safety inspector filing a report during the demolition. In a 1990 Trenton restaurant interview, I asked Sullivan how a project of this size could have been erected in the heart of Manhattan without attracting government job safety inspectors. Sullivan just looked at me. When I widened my eyes to make clear that I wanted an explicit answer, he said, "You know why." When I persisted, anticipating that Sullivan might specify bribes to inspectors, he said that unions and concrete suppliers were not the only areas where Trump's lawyer, Roy Cohn, had influence.

Shortly after Trump called Sullivan, a new demolition crew arrived on the site. They were officially members of Housewreckers Local 95, but there were only fifteen or so unionists among them. Normally, employing non-union workers (in this case, Kaszycki & Sons) at a union work site would prompt an immediate shutdown. But, as federal court documents would later show, the Housewreckers Union was firmly under the control of the mobsters whose consigliere was Roy Cohn, Trump's mentor and lawyer. So the union went along with a scheme to employ non-union workers, cheat them out of their pay, and shortchange the union health and pension funds.

Several simple but clever techniques in filling out records ensured that the union received no written notice of the non-union workers. Not incidentally, those workers were nonetheless required to pay union initiation fees and had union dues deducted from their meager pay, even though (as a federal judge later concluded) they were never actually in the union. Macari, Trump's overseer, testified that he reviewed and approved these documents before paying Kaszycki.

Six Polish workers went to a lawyer named John Szabo for help getting paid. In early April, Macari saw to it that the window washing company Trump hired for the demolition job gave the six men a total of almost $5,000 in back pay. More workers then sought out Szabo. By July, as summer temperatures soared, the unpaid wages came to almost $104,000, even though the rate of pay was under five dollars an hour with no overtime, despite a grueling eighty-four-hour workweek of heavy manual labor.

One day, to keep the workers swinging their sledgehammers, Macari showed up with a wad of cash. Instead of paying the men directly, court papers show, Macari gave the money to the foreman. Anyone who wanted their money had to kick back fifty bucks to the foreman, testimony showed. After that, Macari testified later, he handed cash directly to the Polish Brigade members at least twice.

After the building was taken down, a dissident member of the Housewreckers Union, Harry Diduck, took the brave step of suing the corrupt union, Trump, and an arm of Metropolitan Life Insurance (Trump's financial partner in Trump Tower) for the wages and benefits the Polish Brigade members should have received. Trump insisted he owed nothing and filed motion after motion that delayed the proceedings, which his lawyers characterized as baseless and unfair.

When the trial finally made it to federal court, Trump testified that he had no knowledge that any workers were underpaid, or that the Polish workers lacked hard hats and other safety equipment. Judge Stewart, in a lengthy opinion, found that Trump's testimony lacked credibility. The judge said it would have been easy to identify the Polish workers—they were the only ones on the demolition site without hard hats.

Judge Stewart ruled that Trump had engaged in a conspiracy to cheat the workers of their pay. At the heart of this conspiracy was Trump's violation of his duty of loyalty—also known as fiduciary duty—to the workers and to the union. This "breach involved fraud and the Trump defendants knowingly participated in this breach," Judge Stewart held.

The judge awarded damages of $325,000 plus interest. Trump, who has consistently maintained he acted lawfully, appealed. He later settled. The agreement was sealed, so the amount Trump paid remains unknown. Diduck's dedication to his fellow workers showed amazing persistence—the sealed settlement took effect more than eighteen years after the demolition began.

There was no litigation over the destruction of the bas-relief façades and the valuable entryway grillwork, which Trump had promised to the Metropolitan Museum of Art. A spokesman for Trump who identified himself as John Baron told *The New York Times* that Trump had ordered their destruction. Baron said three appraisers told Trump that the Art Deco sculpture was "without artistic merit." Museum curators, the building's architect, and a host of architectural experts all said that was nonsense.

Baron said removing the art would have cost Trump more than a half million dollars in demolition delays, other unspecified expenses, and (without explanation) additional taxes. That last item may have struck those following the dispute as curious; by donating the art, Trump would have qualified for an income tax deduction. Of course, that deduction would have no value if Trump did not owe any income taxes in 1980, as public records show was the case in 1978 and 1979, and would be again in 1984, 1992, 1994, and likely every other year since 1978.

The entry grillwork that *American Architect* magazine had so highly praised a half-century earlier just vanished. Baron said the grillwork and the limestone panels, if preserved, could not have been sold for more than $9,000. Art experts dismissed that as nonsense as well. The Metropolitan Museum said its twentieth-century art curators never would have requested the donation of objects that lacked artistic merit or had no value in the market. The museum said one appraiser had estimated the value of the art in the hundreds of thousands of dollars. Others called the destroyed artifacts priceless, comparing them to the renowned artwork on the Rockefeller Center buildings.

Otto J. Teegan, who designed the grillwork in 1929, was still alive in 1980. Baron had said the grillwork just disappeared. Teegan wasn't buying that. Teegan and others told the newspaper they were appalled. Teegan said the grille "would have required cranes and trucks to be removed and could not merely be mislaid or easily stolen. It's not a thing you could slip in your coat and walk away with" since the heavy metal grillwork measured fifteen by twenty-five feet.

Trump spoke up days later, saying safety concerns were his real worry, namely the fear of heavy limestone falling onto the sidewalk and street. "My biggest concern was the safety of the people on the street below," he said. "If one of those stones had slipped, people could have been killed. To me, it would not have been worth that kind of risk."

Noted art dealer Robert Miller, who watched the destruction of the limestone sculptures from his gallery across the street, described how huge pieces of stone did in fact crash to the Fifth Avenue sidewalk. "They were just jackhammered in half and pulled down in such a way that they just shattered . . . [I]t was just tragic. They were very much in the Art Deco style—very beautiful and very gracious."

Trump insisted that he was being cheap in destroying the art, rather than preserving it, to save what may have been about $32,000. "I contribute that much every month to painters and artists—that's nothing," Trump said. Years later, as a presidential candidate, Trump would have little evidence to support his claim to being an "ardent philanthropist," as we shall see.

The destruction of the Bonwit Teller artwork, together with the Polish Brigade case, highlighted some of Trump's unscrupulous business practices, but it also brought to light another intriguing aspect of Trump's conduct, one that raises serious questions about the lack of judgment that troubled Daniel Sullivan. For years, Trump used fake identities to mislead journalists—and at least once to menace someone who was just doing their duty. This will be examined after we take a look at some other aspects of Trump, including how emotions influence how much Trump says he is worth.

10

—

FEELINGS AND NET WORTH

Over more than four decades of promoting himself in public, Donald Trump has declared widely varying figures for his net worth. The numbers sometimes differ by billions of dollars in just a matter of days.

In 1990, when his business empire was on the verge of collapse, Trump told me and many other journalists that he was worth $3 billion. He told others $5 billion. I got my hands on a copy of his personal net worth statement that spring, which revealed a much smaller figure. Two months later, a report commissioned by his bankers and introduced in casino regulatory hearings put Trump in the red by almost $300 million.

In spring 2015, as he prepared to run for the Republican presidential nomination, Trump declared his net worth, on different days, to be $8.7 billion, $10 billion, and in one case $11 billion. Just how does Trump arrive at these fluctuating figures? They do not appear to take into account factors as basic as stock prices, changes in real estate values, and interest rates.

Trump's net worth is central to his public persona as a kind of modern Midas. It is so important to him that he sued veteran journalist Tim O'Brien over a net worth estimate in his 2005 book, *TrumpNation*. O'Brien—who has edited my work in *The New York Times*—estimated Trump's worth at $150 million to $250 million, based on documents Trump had shown him and statements from three unnamed sources. Trump's lawsuit said the correct figure was between $5 billion and $6 billion. The lawsuit accused O'Brien of deliberately undervaluing Trump's net worth so he could sell more books, causing irreparable damage to Trump's reputation as a billionaire.

In pursuing the lawsuit, Trump testified under oath about his actual net worth. But his answers were not the dry recitations of asset values minus debts usually found in financial investigations. The testimony was quintessentially Trumpian.

"Mr. Trump, have you always been completely truthful in your public statements about your net worth of properties?" O'Brien's lawyer asked.

"I try," Trump answered.

"Have you ever not been truthful?"

"My net worth fluctuates, and it goes up and down with markets and with attitudes and with feelings, even my own feelings, but I try."

In that statement, attorney Andrew C. Ceresney of Debevoise & Plimpton—who represented both O'Brien and his publisher—found exactly the opening he was looking for.

"Let me just understand that a little bit," Ceresney said. "Let's talk about net worth for a second. You said that the net worth goes up and down based upon your own feelings?"

"Yes," Trump answered. "Even my own feelings, as to where the world is, where the world is going, and that can change rapidly from day to day. Then you have a September

11th, and you don't feel so good about yourself and you don't feel so good about the world and you don't feel so good about New York City. Then you have a year later, and the city is as hot as a pistol. Even months after that it was a different feeling. So yeah, even my own feelings affect my value to myself."

"When you publicly state what you're worth," the lawyer asked, "what do you base that number on?"

"I would say it's my general attitude at the time that the question may be asked. And as I say, it varies," Trump replied.

Trump's answers were a remarkably candid explanation of his behavior, which he modulates in public to polish the careful image of his ability to make money through deal artistry. Whether being under oath prompted his candor or he simply felt relaxed after decades of lawsuits is unknowable. A New Jersey state appeals court, in its 2011 decision dismissing Trump's lawsuit, concluded that Trump's testimony "failed to provide a reliable measure" of his net worth that could be used to impeach O'Brien's reporting. In short, the core issue in Trump's lawsuit was not hard facts and figures, but Trump's feelings. The lawsuit had no basis in reality.

The decision cited a document that O'Brien said Trump showed him three times, the "Statement of Financial Condition prepared by Weiser L.L.P., Certified Public Accountants," as a measure of Trump's fortune. The judge wrote of that problematic document:

A preface to that statement demonstrates its limited value as an accurate representation of Trump's net worth. The accountants cautioned that they had "not audited or reviewed the accompanying statement of financial condition and, accordingly, do not express an opinion or any other form of assurance on it."

Further, the accountants noted significant departures from generally accepted accounting principles,
and stated "[t]he effects of the departures from generally
accepted accounting principles as described above have
not been determined."

Explaining the lack of audit or review, the judge quoted
Gerald Rosenblum, one of the accountants who helped prepare the statement. Rosenblum testified that he did not try to
independently assess Trump's financial condition: "I asked the
client to provide me with a list of liabilities as they existed at
June 30, 2005," said Rosenblum. "The client presented me with
a list, in essence. I'm not certain to this day that I was aware of
all of Mr. Trump's liabilities at that point in time, and I sought
no corroboration."

The ruling said that Trump's right to collect income in the
future was presented as a certainty without regard for the fact
that under the terms of his contracts, the flow of money might
be reduced or even stop.

More important, the judge wrote that Trump had not disclosed facts needed to determine his net worth: "The values of
Trump's closely held businesses were not expressed in terms of
assets or net of liabilities," the judge wrote, before adding two
crucial insights—insights that speak to how Trump could make
his net worth seem to be vastly larger than it is by any standard
objective measure. "The ownership percentages of each closely
held business held by Trump were not disclosed. Additionally,
the tax consequences on Trump's holdings were not set forth."

The court also took renewed interest in Trump's stake in
the West Side Yards in Manhattan, which more than three
decades earlier had been the focus of a federal grand jury investigation in which Trump was a target. No charges were

filed. The New Jersey judge's dismissal order held that the West Side Yards, the largest single piece of land available for development in Manhattan, was not "owned" by Trump, as he often claimed. Rather, as *TrumpNation* reported, Trump was subject to a partnership agreement with terms that might not be worth a dollar to him. Under oath, Trump admitted that, in the judge's words, "under the partnership agreement, the general partners would have to recover their entire investment before Trump would see any return. As a consequence, his future profits remained speculative." Any possible future profits are uncertain "because encumbrances on the property were not disclosed by Trump."

As often as Trump overstates his properties' worth, the judge's decision also points to how he also understates or even hides debts and other liabilities or encumbrances, like mortgages. In 1985, Trump made a show of buying Mar-a-Lago, the Palm Beach, Florida, estate of Marjorie Merriweather Post, the cereal heiress who went on to run her own cereal company and became arguably the wealthiest woman in America. Post left the property to the federal government in 1973 as a winter home for the president, but Washington decided the upkeep of more than 110,000 square feet with 126 rooms and lavish grounds was more than taxpayers should bear. They put it on the market.

Trump said he paid cash for the property, which he described as run-down and in need of the Trump touch to restore its grandeur. No mortgage was involved, he said, just cash. "I put in a cash offer of five million, plus another three million for the furnishings in the house," Trump wrote in his first book.

That was not quite true. In testimony five years later, Trump confirmed that his primary bank, Chase Manhattan, had loaned him the entire purchase price.

"They put up the eight million dollars, I believe it was eight million purchase price," Trump testified.

"Was there any security given to Chase Manhattan for that?" the lawyer asked, inquiring as to whether a mortgage had been taken out to finance the purchase and secure the bank's interest.

"It's a mortgage, a non-recorded mortgage," said Trump. "And because it's non-recorded, I personally guaranteed it."

In December 1985, Trump had written to Janet VB Pena, a second vice president of Chase Manhattan, seeking several modifications to the mortgage commitment the bank had made two weeks earlier. The mortgage "will not be recorded" unless Trump failed to make timely payments, a condition the bank accepted.

The bank loaned Trump $2 million more than the purchase price, a total of $10 million, on his personal guarantee. Trump put up only $2,800 cash. He boasted that he got Mar-a-Lago for a song, a bargain that showed his extraordinary negotiating skills. "I've been told the furnishings in Mar-A-Lago alone are worth more than what I paid for the house," he said in his book.

To local property tax authorities, Trump represented the situation differently. They put a value of $11.5 million on the land and buildings. Trump countered, saying that was far too much. Keeping up the estate would cost him $2 million or $2.5 million a year, he said, so he might have to subdivide and develop the land. He proposed to build ten small mansions on the grounds. The town council turned him down. Then he proposed seven mansions. Turned down again. He would have to settle for building some condos nearby.

Five years after Trump acquired Mar-a-Lago with the unrecorded mortgage, casino regulatory hearings revealed that he had personally guaranteed more than a fourth of his more than $3 billion of debt. Many banks complained that they were unaware other banks had loaned money to Trump on his personal guarantee with no public record of the obligation.

Taking wildly different positions on the value of assets and using his emotional state to justify those valuations helps explain something else Trump has done repeatedly. Congress requires all presidential candidates to file a financial disclosure statement listing their assets, liabilities, and income. Trump's ninety-two-page disclosure report valued one of his best-known properties at more than $50 million. But he told tax authorities the same property was worth only about $1 million. He valued another signature Trump property at zero—and demanded the return of the property taxes he had already paid.

11

—

GOVERNMENT RESCUES TRUMP

n the years between 1986 and the spring of 1990, Donald
Trump took in at least $375.2 million from his business enter-
prises. He got cash from real estate deals. He made profits
through greenmailing. He took $90.5 million out of Atlantic
City, stripping cash from his Trump's Castle and Trump Plaza
casinos. His recorded cash flow averaged $1.6 million per week
for 233 weeks. That's $230,000 per day, nearly $10,000 per hour,
$160 a minute, or $2.66 per second.

Yet, in the spring of 1990, Donald Trump could not pay his
bills. How could a man who had convinced the world he was a
multibillionaire fail to pay contractors on his new Trump Taj
Mahal—which opened April 5, 1990—for months after they
had completed their work? How could he lack the resources
to make a $73 million mortgage payment on Trump's Castle
Casino Resort by the Bay?

The $375.2 million was not pure profit, by any means.
Out of it came fees to lawyers and investment bankers, and
interest paid on stock acquired with borrowed money. But

neither does the figure include cash generated by his other investments—for which no reliable public figures exist. For example, independent observers in 1990 said Trump had received millions of dollars in developer fees and operating profits from three Manhattan buildings—the Grand Hyatt Hotel, Trump Tower, and Trump Parc—but no one knows just how much. All we have to go on are Trump's many and often conflicting claims.

Despite Trump's tremendous cash flow over those four years, Manhattan bankers occupied a Trump Tower conference room for more than a month in 1990 as he dickered with them for more loans to keep his empire afloat. Trump's inability to pay his debts had put him at risk of losing his casinos. The New Jersey Casino Control Act required that a casino owner be able to pay bills as they came due. If an owner could not pay a bill, he or she was out. If an owner could not pay cash, but could convince a creditor to extend the payment date, that was fine. Old loans could be paid off with proceeds from new loans. But unpaid bills were cause for the Casino Control Commission to cancel the casino ownership license, take control of the casino, and have it run by trustees until a buyer was approved.

The law put the onus on Trump to establish his financial stability by "clear and convincing evidence." Nearly two decades before Congress decided that America's top banks were too big to fail, New Jersey debated whether the same applied to one self-proclaimed multibillionaire. If the answer was yes, then Donald Trump needed a government rescue to keep his empire intact.

At the time, Trump told me and everybody else that he was worth $3 billion. It was a dubious claim for a simple reason: in

February 1990, Trump had quit paying many of his personal bills.

A few weeks later, I got my hands on Trump's personal financial statement, which showed that he expected his income to fall to $748,000 in 1992 and to $296,000 in 1993. That's a lot of money to most people, but not to a "billionaire" with a personal jet to maintain.

My *Philadelphia Inquirer* piece broke the news that whatever Trump was worth, he was no billionaire, much less the multibillionaire he repeatedly claimed to be. Soon after that news story, casino regulators publicized a document showing that Trump was down to his last $1.6 million. Yet payments on more than $1 billion worth of bonds on his three Atlantic City casinos came due every ninety days.

About a hundred vendors at the newly opened Trump Taj Mahal casino took legal action to protect their interests, filing liens and other debt-protection documents. The Trump Shuttle airline that ferried passengers between Boston, New York City, and Washington was burning cash at a furious rate. Trump said the planes had gold sinks and seat-belt buckles, but the Shuttle was down to $1 million cash. That was not enough to pay employees, keep the fleet of Boeing 727s fueled, or pay for constant repairs (which were necessary, since all but one of the twenty-three airplanes were more than twenty years old).

Trump's obvious difficulty complying with the financial stability requirements of the Casino Control Act raised a glaring question: Had the regulators been monitoring Trump's finances since he got his casino license in 1982? The answer was no.

The regulators had been too busy with work they deemed more important. There was, for example, the predawn arrest of a cocktail waitress named Diane Pussehl, who was pulled from bed and charged with a felony for picking up a $500 chip on the floor of Harrah's casino. A judge tossed the case out, so the casino regulators filed a misdemeanor charge. It also was tossed. Then they went after Pussehl's license, arguing she was morally unfit to work in a casino. Pussehl kept her license.

The Division of Gaming Enforcement came down like a wall of bricks on little people like Pussehl, but when it came to high-level regulation—casino owners playing financial games with customers connected to the Medellín drug cartel, or accusations by Trump's biggest customer, Bob Libutti, of manipulating financial reports on the purchase of gambling chips—the regulators remained willfully blind. It was the perfect environment for a Trump.

But Trump's unpaid bills and the presence of all those bankers in Trump Tower made it impossible for the Division of Gaming Enforcement to keep its blinders on. As more and more news reports showed the financial stress Trump was under, the DGE said it would investigate.

The seventy banks whose massive loans were about to sour insisted that Trump install a man they trusted in his headquarters: Steven F. Bollenbach, who would later head Hilton Hotels and become chief financial officer at Disney. Bollenbach had experience with Trump. In 1987, on his first day as chief financial officer at the Holiday Corporation—the owner of the Holiday Inn brand and Trump's original partner in the Trump Plaza casino—Trump attempted to greenmail that company. Bollenbach directed Holiday's successful effort to fend off Trump.

Bollenbach spent days in a Trump office reading through contracts, loan papers, and other documents. To use phrases that Trump would employ a quarter century later on the campaign trail, Bollenbach's duty was to "figure out what the hell is going on."

In March, Trump filed a sworn statement with the Casino Control Commission listing his net worth at $1.5 billion, half of his previous public proclamations. Meanwhile, the seventy banks hired the Kenneth Leventhal & Co. accounting firm to go over Trump's books. An independent evaluation of Trump's finances was crucial. While the big New York banks agreed to advance Trump $60 million to avoid a fire sale of his assets, not all the banks were on board. Three Japanese banks—Sumitomo, Mitsubishi, and Dai-Ichi Kangyo—plus the German Dresdner Bank were balking, as were two smaller New Jersey banks, First Fidelity and Midlantic. The agreement required every bank to go along or the deal would fail. Ultimately all but Dresdner did. Since none of the banks trusted Trump, the objective Leventhal evaluation was central to understanding the actual state of Trump's finances.

The Leventhal report showed that Trump was no billionaire: he had a net worth of minus $295 million. My story on that report ran across the front page of the *Philadelphia Inquirer* with the headline: "Bankers Say Trump May Be Worth Less Than Zero." The lead sentence was, "You may well be worth more than Donald Trump."

Trump hated that line and the traction the story received. The story ran at a critical moment in Trump's bid to keep his casinos. He could have been swept into the dustbin of history if the DGE prosecuted high-level offenders with the same rigor as it did the Diane Pussehl of the industry. Instead, the Casino Control Commission listened to a less than vigorous challenge to Trump's financial stability. Thomas Auriemma, the DGE lawyer, asked Trump's representatives easy and irrelevant questions to gloss over the growing gap between the revenue Trump was taking in and the bills he had coming due. The Leventhal accounting firm's report showed that Trump's financial situation was deteriorating rapidly. Instead of ending the year with $24 million in cash, Trump was expected to run dry before year's end.

The DGE prepared its own 111-page report. It noted that Trump owed (not owned, but owed) $3.2 billion. Of that, he had personally guaranteed $833.5 million. Absent an agreement by all creditors, Trump would face an uncontrolled, domino-effect chain of bankruptcies. If just one creditor moved against one Trump property, the others would follow, creating chaos.

More than one thousand lawyers working for Trump and his creditors had hammered out a "fragile" deal to keep him going, hoping to minimize losses on the loans they had extended without checking his finances carefully. The lawyers had already billed almost $11 million for their services.

Part of the deal was putting Trump on an allowance. He would have to get by on $450,000 per month, down from his May 1990 spending of $583,000 (the equivalent of more than one million 2016 dollars). The allowance was so astonishingly large that *The New York Times* quoted one billionaire as saying, "I would have no idea how to spend $450,000 a month. It's just phenomenal."

In order to prevent the legal chaos that would result from a complete collapse of the debt-laden Trump empire, the deal required fast approval by at least four of the five Casino Control Commission members. When two commissioners began asking skeptical questions, Trump attorney Nick Ribis called for a break. The dozen reporters in the front row stood up as the commission adjourned, a few looking bewildered. Why were they taking a break now instead of finishing?

"They're rehearsing the answer to the next question," I advised my colleagues. "When they come back, they'll have the witness say Trump will be torn apart by the bankers unless the commission votes immediate approval of his deal with them."

The one word I knew would not be spoken was *bankrupt.* That's why they needed to rehearse: to convey the idea of bankruptcy without saying the word, which Trump had prohibited. The press-savvy Trump knew that the word *bankrupt* would provide easy headlines for his two favorite New York papers—*Post* and the *Daily News*—but subtle wording would pass over the heads of most journalists. He was soon proved right.

After the recess, Thomas Cerabino, a Trump lawyer at the center of the private bankruptcy negotiations, took the stand.

"What would happen if the commission delayed approving the deal between Trump and his bankers?" asked the DGE's lawyer, Thomas Auriemma.

"I think there would be an imminent risk of the collapse [of the deal]," Cerabino responded.

One of the two skeptical commissioners asked for clarification: What would happen if the commission delayed immediate approval?

Cerabino testified in slow, deliberate words: "The banks will move apart and take whatever steps they think are appropriate to protect their interests and that is a very unhealthy state affairs for the Trump Organizations."

With the lawyers' subtle language, Trump avoided the "B" word but made clear to the commissioners that an uncontrolled bankruptcy was one day away. *The Philadelphia Inquirer* again bannered the story, this time with the headline, "Trump Empire Could Tumble Today, Casino Panel Told."

All but two of the other reporters who had been told what testimony to expect missed the story. Because the word *bankruptcy* went unsaid, these reporters did not allude to it.

Many reporters accurately quote what they are told, but don't know much about the underlying issues. For Trump and others like him, this makes it easy to manipulate most of the press. Those who see through that manipulation and make connections themselves get a different response: complaints to editors, threats of litigation, and occasionally public denunciations. That latter strategy was on display the next day before the hearings resumed.

When I arrived, several reporters rushed up to me, one clutching my big front-page headline, asking when I would retract my story. They said that Ribis, Trump's casino lawyer, had just told them my story was wrong, completely wrong. I marched over to Ribis, asked a series of short questions whose answers established that my story was correct, and had him confirm to my peers that no retraction or even correction would be requested.

When the commissioners entered the room, they faced a choice. They could approve the "fragile deal" with the banks or go with the evidence showing that Trump was financially unstable and rescind his license.

Four of the five commissioners, all political appointees, used their power to take Trump's side. The commission told the bankers they were free to foreclose on Trump. However, the casino licenses would not ride with the foreclosures. Without the casinos, the banks would repossess gigantic hotels with no reason to stay in business, leaving them far worse off than if they went along with the deal. That deal would 1) allow Trump to pay them back less than he owed and 2) advance him $60 million to keep going.

Donald Trump was saved—saved by the government, deeming him too big to fail—from getting his just desserts for reckless spending. The state of New Jersey had favored the interests of Trump over those of his bankers and the people who invested in those banks.

Years later, running for president, Trump would make remarks that seemed to harken back to this day, although he did not mention it specifically. In the spring of 2016, Trump told CNBC: "I've borrowed knowing that you can pay back with discounts. And I've done very well with debt. Now, of course, I was swashbuckling, and it did well for me, and it was good for me and all that."

Even with the official favoritism that forgave many of Trump's debts, he was still in financial trouble. As Christmas 1990 approached, Trump was again running out of cash. Many of the Taj Mahal contractors remained unpaid, as they would for years or, in some cases, forever. It was the beginning of Trump being forced to relinquish his stakes in a host of enterprises.

In 1991, the Trump Taj Mahal entered Chapter 11 bankruptcy, the first of his business bankruptcies. He later sold stock in his casinos, where investors lost their shirts (while Trump kept getting paid millions of dollars in salary, bonuses, and money to pay off his bad debts). During the fourth bankruptcy case, creditors successfully demanded that Trump get lost.

Today, Trump shrugs off the four bankruptcies in which investors lost more than $1.5 billion, saying it's a standard business tactic to restructure debt. In truth, there were actually six bankruptcies. The last was in 2014, when Trump was a very minor investor in the Trump Taj; he had already been removed from any active role in the last casino bearing his name.

In 1990, Trump feared the word *bankruptcy* as he now fears damning questions from Hugh Hewitt or Megyn Kelly, the Fox News host. If government hadn't saved him by taking his side against his bankers, we almost certainly would not be imagining the prospect of Donald Trump living at 1600 Pennsylvania Avenue. Instead, he would have drowned in a sea of red ink.

12

—

GOLF AND TAXES

ike his father before him, Trump has often placed wildly variable values on his properties in official documents, presenting high values to bankers, investors, and the public (including when he donates property to charity), and small numbers to tax authorities, contractors, and vendors seeking payment for work. Government auditors, bankers, and investors have questioned these mismatches on multiple occasions. In every case that has been resolved, Trump has negotiated civil settlements, many on undisclosed terms. Judges sealed these files.

Of Trump's fifteen golf courses, his Federal Election Commission disclosure form values nine of them at more than $50 million. "Golf is a small part of my business," Trump told golf writer Michael Bamberger in 2011. "One, two percent. But you know why I spend so much time on it? Because I do what I want and I like it."

Among Trump's top-valued properties is the Trump National Golf Club Westchester, about thirty miles from Trump Tower in the prosperous town of Briarcliff Manor. Homes in Briarcliff Manor typically sell for three-quarters of a million dollars. In the 1990s, Trump bought a failed golf course there. He beautified and developed it. He built a clubhouse with one and a quarter acres of floor space that he said cost $20 million. Trump boasted that "no expense was spared" in creating a "world-class" golf course. He built a majestic 101-foot-high waterfall and added numerous man-made ponds.

Bill Clinton, who owns a home six miles away, is among those who have paid the club's initiation fee, reported to be about $300,000. Trump has testified under oath that annual revenues from golfing, weddings, and other events at Trump National Golf Club Westchester total $9.5 million.

While Trump declared (also under oath) that more than $50 million is the "true, complete, and correct" value of this golf course, he told Fernando Gonzalez otherwise when formally challenging his property tax bill. Gonzalez is the property tax assessor for Briarcliff Manor. In that instance, Trump lowered his appraisal of the golf club to less than $1.4 million. Two average Briarcliff Manor homes cost about that much.

Modest differences in property values are routine. Assessors often hold hearings for appeals on the property tax valuations they assign. In property tax appeals, the difference between a valuation and an appeal is usually no more than a few percentage points. The difference between what Trump swore in his Federal Election Commission filings and his property tax appeal was 97 percent.

After David McKay Wilson, a watchdog reporter for the local *Gannett* newspaper and ABC News' Brian Ross reported on the chasm between assessments, Trump upped his valuation of the golf course to about $9 million, still less than a fifth of what he swore to be the true value as a presidential candidate.

Trump's appeal annoyed the locals, who would have to make up for the reduced tax bill he'd receive. Richard Wishnie, a former Westchester County legislator who lives in Briarcliff Manor, said it "makes no sense to me for any of us to subsidize a billionaire so he can enjoy even more profits at that property."

Cutting his property tax bill was not the only thing that had irritated locals. Trump has also refused to pay the town for damage it says was caused by runoff from the golf course after a series of storms drenched the area in June 2011. Water flooded the municipal swimming pool, leaving a thick layer of silt. The city said Trump had made "unauthorized alterations" to water outlets at five golf course ponds, raising the water level as much as six feet to make them more attractive, leaving no room to capture water from heavy downpours.

According to court documents filed by Briarcliff Manor when Trump wouldn't pay for the mess, "the failure of the Trump storm water facilities to perform as designed was the sole direct cause of the village damage." Alan Garten, general counsel for the Trump Organization, denied any responsibility and told Wilson that "local taxpayers would end up suffering from the legal battle." Garten blamed the flooding primarily on a drainage pipe that "was clogged because the village was too cheap to put up a grate to prevent rocks and boulders from coming in." Garten further accused town officials of "letting their egos get in the way. It's not the best use of taxpayer dollars." The litigation remained unresolved when this book was completed in July 2016.

• • •

The Westchester golf course is not the only one about which Trump's property tax filing and campaign disclosure reports are at odds.

In the rolling open hills of Bedminster, New Jersey, Trump acquired the former farm of John Z. DeLorean, creator of the eponymous steel car and defendant in a much-publicized drug-trafficking trial that ended in his acquittal. Trump bought the 580 acres out of bankruptcy for what he said was "far less" than the actual $34 million that was spent buying the land and starting work on the golf course, a discount that enhanced his future return in the investment.

He christened it the Trump National Golf Club Bedminster. World-class golf course architects Tom Fazio and son designed the course. Trump's daughter Ivanka was married there in 2009, and it might be Trump's final resting place. He sought permission for a cemetery for ten people, but a special deal zoned ten acres of the property as a future cemetery for almost three hundred souls, exempting them from property taxes.

In his campaign disclosures, Trump valued his National Golf Club Bedminster at more than $50 million and said it had annual revenues of more than $16 million. For that valuation to be accurate, it would have to be calculated after Trump gave away the rights to develop the land (with, for example, housing or retail). To this end, Trump signed what is known as a land conservation easement. No cash changed hands, but the value of the property was reduced in exchange for being preserved as an open space—in this case, in the form of a golf course. Public documents indicate that this entitled Trump to an income tax deduction of $39.1 million.

For property tax purposes, assessors make separate determinations of value for the parcels that make up the old DeLorean estate. Bedminster Township tax records show the golf club land and buildings to be valued (for property tax purposes) at $32.3 million. The property tax in 2015 was just under $440,000 at a property tax rate of 1.4 percent, well below the statewide average of 2.2 percent. On part of the property, Trump nearly wipes out his property tax bill by penning in a small herd of goats. Without the goats, the bill would be $80,000 a year, but because the goats qualify it as active farmland, the tax comes to just under $1,100.

Trump has also offered widely varying values of his California golf course. The Trump National Golf Club Los Angeles—located on the Palos Verdes Peninsula overlooking the Pacific Ocean—opened in 2006. Trump and his publicists said the golfing property was worth more than a quarter of a billion dollars. News reports blindly accepted that figure, even though public records show that Trump paid only $27 million when he bought the old Ocean Trails Golf Course after the eighteenth hole slid into the ocean in 1999. Trump's 2015 presidential disclosure form lists the value only as "more than" $50 million.

Yet despite this impressive valuation, Trump filed papers with the Los Angeles County assessor valuing the golf course at a humble $10 million, less than four cents on the dollar of his highest public statements.

Trump gained property tax and income tax breaks on the Palos Verdes property by giving away his right to build luxury homes on the land—another conservation easement like the one in Bedminster Township. His disclosure papers value the Palos Verdes easement at $26 million.

That is an exceptionally high value to place on land that can never be developed.

Locals knew, as did Trump and anyone with a basic grasp of geology, that land on this part of the Palos Verdes Peninsula is unstable and therefore not suitable for development. The

acres Trump identified in the easement shift frequently because of fault lines and unstable soil. The continual land move-
ments sometimes force the closure of Palos Verdes Drive, the
curving road that winds along the water's edge. Even when
the roadway is open to traffic, the shifting land forces drivers
on parts of the road to navigate around asphalt moguls.

Trump tried to develop the land anyway, only to be told no
by Palos Verdes officials. In 2008, Trump sued the town for $100
million, more than five times the town's annual budget. Showing his relish for litigation, Trump told the *Los Angeles Times*:
"I've been looking forward for a long time to do this." The
case was settled four years later, the terms sealed by a judge.

Land unsuitable for development generally has little or
no value. In this case, the supposed development rights that
Trump gave away when he signed the easement on the land
almost equaled the price he paid for it. Federal and state tax
auditors, if they questioned this, would likely have approved
no deduction for the development rights since the land would
not support structures. But Trump's surrender of development
rights included a strong element of self-interest: The site was
not maintained as an open field to preserve the sweeping views
of the ocean and Catalina Island, twenty-six miles across the
sea. The land is used as a driving-range annex to his golf course.

Trump took an even stronger view of how little his real
estate is worth in a series of Chicago property tax appeals. In
this case, he turned for help to Edward M. Burke, a local Democratic Party power who has been a Chicago city alderman
since 1969. Burke's law firm also handles appeals against city
property tax assessments. Having friends in powerful places
(rather than fighting with local officials, as Trump did in Palos
Verdes) can pay off.

•   •   •

Trump International Hotel & Tower soars more than 1,300 feet above the north side of the Chicago River and stands as the second tallest building in the Windy City, the fourth tallest in America. It cost Trump $847 million to buy the land, tear down the old *Chicago Sun-Times* newspaper building, and erect the concrete high-rise. Trump testified in an unrelated lawsuit that he owns it all, except for the individual condominium apartments he has sold.

On Trump's behalf, Alderman Burke won tax discounts that cut the Trump Organization's property tax bills by almost $12 million, a reduction of 39 percent. *Chicago Sun-Times* reporters Tim Novak and Chris Fusco calculated this discount after examining more than 1,500 property tax bills sent to the building and distilling those that were Trump's responsibility from those that went to individual apartment owners. Further still, Trump had Alderman Burke sue the public schools, the city, the county, and other taxing authorities for refunds of "erroneous, excessive, illegal" taxes. The suit claimed that the taxes were so egregiously high that they should have been voided and the taxes already paid fully refunded.

Also intriguing is the value applied to the retail space at Trump International: $75 million after the tower opened in 2009. Kelly Keeling Hahn, a lawyer at Alderman Burke's firm, wrote, "The hotel is NOT located in the prime Michigan Avenue hotel area," adding that "the entire retail space of the building is unleasable." Indeed, the retail space is empty, a mix of rubble and dirt floors that was never completed because it violates the three basic rules of real estate investment: location, location, location. Not only is the retail space a hike from the Miracle Mile, it is also on the wrong side of the Chicago River; the city had decided even before Trump came along that its focus would be on the south side.

Assuming that Hahn's letter is an accurate statement of the facts, how could Trump have become involved with such a total loser of an investment, especially given his endlessly repeated claims of exceptional prowess as a businessman and real estate investor? How could he have failed to notice that the tower bearing his name in huge letters was not on Michigan Avenue's Magnificent Mile, where high-end retailers flourish?

The assessor slashed the retail space property tax valuation by almost $49 million, a 65 percent reduction. It is unclear whether Hahn's letter was persuasive in securing the lower value. Trump has often boasted (in the past and on the campaign trail) that he buys the friendship of politicians so they "do what I want." The Republican presidential hopeful made sure he would have Chicago friends in powerful places by making nearly $100,000 in campaign contributions to local politicians—all of them Democrats.

A new Cook County assessor has sought to increase Trump Tower property tax assessments on the hotel and other spaces in active use. Trump has continued to seek lower assessments, perhaps reflecting his inability to charge high rates for hotel rooms because of its out-of-the-way location and the squeamishness some corporations and retailers have developed about associating their brands with Trump since his latest candidacy.

But asserting that the properties he calls top-shelf in one forum are virtually worthless in others is not Trump's only technique for avoiding taxes. He also works hard to avoid income taxes and has even reported huge directions from a business that had no revenue.

13

—

INCOME TAXES

For more than two decades beginning in the early 1970s, Jack Mitnick prepared Donald Trump's income tax returns. An NYU-educated lawyer and certified public accountant, Mitnick also handled appeals when Trump felt his income taxes were unfair. That included two tax appeals in 1984, a year in which Trump collected many millions of dollars but paid no federal income tax.

Mitnick has testified that he is "thoroughly familiar" with every aspect of Trump's finances. In *The Art of the Deal*, Trump recounts a typical conversation with Mitnick about the tax implications of a deal he was working on as it related to the 1986 Tax Reform Act that President Reagan had just signed into law, shutting down a host of tax shelters. Trump wrote that he expected the new tax law to be a disaster for the country, especially real estate investors. "To my surprise, Mitnick tells me he thinks the law is an overall plus for me," Trump wrote.

Trump and Mitnick were close, and Trump had done well

following his accountant's advice. In 1978, the newlywed Trump lived lavishly, but paid no federal income taxes. He didn't pay in 1979 either, thanks to Mitnick's understanding of special tax rules for large real estate investors.

The fact that Trump paid no tax came to light when casino regulators issued a public report on his fitness to own a casino. Trump's tax returns showed negative income. That's because Congress lets big real estate investors offset their income from salaries, stock market gains, consulting fees, and other income with losses from depreciation in the value of their buildings. If these paper losses for the declining value of their buildings are greater than their cash income from other sources, real estate investors can legally tell the IRS that their income is less than zero and no federal income tax is due.

Trump's 1978 tax return reported a negative income of $406,379. In 1979, his income went negative by more than $3.4 million. During a lunch interview one day in 1990, I suggested to Trump that he could become a little richer by reorganizing his various partnerships so that his income was negative by only about one dollar. That would be enough to wipe out income taxes; larger losses were pure waste. Trump seemed nonplussed that a journalist understood tax law, but he thanked me.

Two years later, in 1992, Mitnick represented Trump when hearings were finally held on appeals from two earlier tax audits. Both the City and the State of New York had audited Trump's 1984 income tax returns. Both concluded that Trump owed more tax. Trump told Mitnick to fight.

The year made famous by George Orwell's novel was Trump's best ever to that point. Millions of dollars flowed into his accounts, a Niagara of greenbacks. Early that year, Trump and others moved into apartments at Trump Tower, which meant millions of dollars from the sale of apartments on forty-four floors. Trump also collected rent for retail and office spaces on the nine lower floors of Trump Tower, which were pricey even for Fifth Avenue. In May, his first casino opened in Atlantic City, catching the full summer gambling season. Players lost millions of dollars at his tables and slot machines.

New York is known as a "strict federal" income state, meaning that except for some income that senior citizens collect free of state tax, the entries on an individual's federal tax return should match their state return. Trump's federal tax return included a Schedule C, the form used by freelancers and other sole proprietors whose businesses are neither corporations nor partnerships. He also included a New York State sole proprietor return and a City return for unincorporated business. Trump identified his business title not as real estate developer or even casino owner, but as consultant.

Trump's return showed zero income from this consulting business. Normally, one would not file a Schedule C without income, but Trump's return showed huge deductions. His federal return deducted $626,400 of expenses. The city form listed a slightly smaller amount: deductions of $619,227 against zero income. That prompted New York City and State auditors to independently flag Trump's tax return for scrutiny. The city asked for evidence that the sole proprietor deductions were legitimate.

Taxpayers do not have to substantiate deductions when they file their tax returns. That is why tax returns include an oath, known as a jurat. The federal jurat states: "Under penalties of perjury, I declare that I have examined this return and accompanying schedules and statements, and to the best of my knowledge and belief, they are true, correct, and complete." Auditors, on the other hand, require substantiation.

The auditors asked that Trump document his large deductions. Trump provided nothing. Not one receipt, invoice, or cleared check. In that case, the auditors said, the deductions were denied. They billed Trump for the taxes he avoided by taking the huge deductions he could not substantiate. Interest was added. So were penalties, a civil law technique used to discourage tax cheating. The penalties came to 35 percent at the state level and 25 percent at the city level.

Trump appealed. Mitnick argued his case. During a city appeal hearing that stretched over two days in 1992, Mitnick provided no documentation to support the deductions. H. Gregory Tillman, the Harvard-educated judge hearing the appeal, noted this extraordinary testimony in his decision. He also noted, "The record does not explain how Petitioner [Trump] had significant expenses without any concomitant income from his consulting business."

Mitnick was shown Trump's tax returns. He verified that his signature was on the document in front of him, but then added a very strange statement about himself and his firm:

"We did not" prepare that return, Mitnick testified.

If Mitnick (who has a clean record with the state bar) was telling the truth, then who prepared that return? The only person who would benefit from filing the document would be Donald J. Trump. With a photocopy machine, one person's name can be transferred to a document they did not prepare. Decades ago, my first national investigative reporting award was for exposing just such a deception.

The court opinion does not address how Mitnick's signature ended up on the photocopy of a return he said he did not prepare. The appeals records, except for Tillman's decision, were destroyed—a routine procedure—years ago. I asked Mitnick in 2016 about his testimony. He said he did not remember it. It is likely to remain a mystery how what appeared to be Mitnick's signature got onto the return.

Tillman found no factual basis for Trump's unsubstantiated deductions. He also noted that Trump's complaint, without explanation, was that he had been subjected to double taxation of his income. Using boldface typeface, which is rare in judicial opinions, Tillman wrote, "The problem at issue is not one of **double taxation**, but of **no taxation**."

Tillman ruled against Trump. However, he waived the 25 percent penalty for underreporting income because no original City tax return could be located, only the photocopy in the city's files with Mitnick's evidently forged signature.

Then came the state case. Here, too, Trump could not produce any documentation supporting the way he accounted for profits from apartments sold at the Trump Plaza at 167 East 61st Street in Manhattan. Frank W. Barrie, an administrative law judge, wrote in his twenty-three-page opinion that Trump "failed to substantiate [Trump's] entitlement" to the tax savings he sought. The judge, underlining the word *not*, ruled that Trump had not established the most basic facts required to justify paying less tax.

Also at issue was whether Trump had filed tax appeal papers before the legal deadline. The judge said that Trump's "mere allegation that [his] failure was due to reasonable cause and not due to willful neglect is inadequate to shoulder such burden."

Judge Barrie then turned to the 35 percent penalty recommended by the state tax auditor, which they said was mandatory under state law given Trump's conduct. "There is nothing in the record, other than the fact that petitioner relied on an attorney/CPA for gains tax advice [which may be implied from Mr. Mitnick's testimony] relevant to the issue of penalty," Judge Barrie wrote. "Consequently the penalty is upheld."

Mitnick, again the sole witness for Trump, "testified that Mr. Trump had no income tax due against which the credit 'could have been applied.'" Barrie ruled that Trump owed the tax as well as interest and a 35 percent penalty.

Asked about those cases in 2016, Mitnick told me he had no memory of them.

The year 1984 was not the last time Trump paid no income tax. The New Jersey Division of Gaming Enforcement, in reports about Trump's financial stability in 1991 and 1993, showed that he had no income tax obligations in those years. The reports also indicated that he had losses so large that he could apply them to future tax seasons. The losses, known as net operating losses (or NOLs), meant that he likely would not owe any taxes for an unspecified number of future years.

In the early 1990s, Congress undid one of the 1986 Tax Reform Act provisions—the one that had troubled Trump. Congress reinstated a tax rule allowing real estate professionals who manage their property to take unlimited deductions against their other income. That means the paper loss from the supposed declining value of a building as it ages could offset other income, such as a salary, profits from golf courses, or fees accrued from selling neckties made in China. However, Congress retained a rule denying these benefits to anyone making more than $150,000 per year and allowing those who make less to offset no more than $25,000 of their other income with paper losses from depreciating buildings they own.

The reinstated tax provision, which benefitted Trump because it applied only to full-time real estate investors who manage their own properties, meant that legally Trump would not pay income taxes, provided he had enough depreciation to offset his other income. Trump would likely have that much depreciation every year, assuming that the value of his buildings is indeed as high as listed on the financial disclosure form he filed as a candidate for president.

Let's take Trump at his word to illustrate how the tax system works for big real estate developers. Trump says NBC paid him $65 million for *Celebrity Apprentice* in both 2011 and 2012 (NBC, in a written statement, said that figure was wildly inflated). If Trump were indeed paid that much, his federal income tax bill would have been almost $23 million. However, if Trump had $65 million or more of depreciation in his buildings, he would report zero income on his tax return. That means he would pay not millions in taxes, but nothing.

The tax bill is not wiped out, however. Under the rules set by Congress, the tax is deferred into the future. The $23 million is therefore the economic equivalent of a loan from Uncle Sam at zero interest. Someday, that loan must be paid off. Typically, real estate partnerships last two decades, so let's assume that Trump invests those loan proceeds for twenty years and earns an annual net return of 10 percent (a return that Trump would consider modest and below his skill level as an investor). When time came to repay his loan, Trump would write the Treasury a check for the almost $23 million and keep his investment gains: $130 million. In this way, Congress further enriches people like Trump, people who have the capital to go into real estate and qualify for tax exemptions under rules that exclude nearly all of their fellow Americans.

This was by no means the last time tax authorities would tangle with Trump. These cases involved his business activities, but another facet of his active efforts to avoid taxes would soon come before a grand jury. It was a case that could have cost him his lucrative casino license.

14

—

EMPTY BOXES

n 1983, after shopping at Bulgari, the high-end jewelry store on Manhattan's posh Fifth Avenue, Donald Trump had a $50,000 necklace mailed to him at an out-of-state address. On another day, he bought jewelry that cost $15,000. It, too, was mailed out of state, sent to the Connecticut home of his mentor and lawyer, the notorious Roy Cohn.

Both boxes were empty.

Mailing empty boxes is a way to evade sales taxes on jewelry, furs, and other expensive items easily shipped through the mail. Under New York law, as in most other states, a visitor who buys goods and has them shipped to her home state does not have to pay New York sales tax. In theory, the buyers then owe an equivalent tax to their home state, known as a use tax, but that levy is only lightly enforced. It was almost never enforced in 1983.

Once New York sales tax auditors got privy to this scam, it was easy to find the tax evaders. They did not have to comb through every individual receipt for the twenty-eight-month period, ending in March 1983, that the investigation covered. In its shipping logs, Bulgari had put an asterisk next to the name of every customer who received an empty box. Then, to save a little bit of money, Bulgari affixed only enough postage to cover the cost of mailing the empty box, not the weight of the jewelry. The jewelry would have only added a few ounces to most of the boxes, but—as the grand jury learned—some of the boxes would have weighed pounds.

Trump was not the only customer named in the investigation. Among the empty box recipients were singer Frank Sinatra, former secretary of state Henry Kissinger, billionaire corporate takeover specialist Ronald Perelman, socialite C. Z. Guest, actress Mary Tyler Moore, and television game show producer Mark Goodson. The investigation, like so many involving the rich or politically powerful, was conducted quietly, with no public announcement, major media coverage, or disclosures of the names of the customers under scrutiny. The story was broken by William Bastone, then a young reporter at the weekly *Village Voice*, learning his craft under future Trump biographer Wayne Barrett.

Bastone identified one additional buyer—Adnan Khashoggi, the Saudi Arabian arms dealer, described at the time as possibly the world's richest man. Khashoggi often partied with Trump, both in New York and Atlantic City. He ducked $17,000 in sales taxes by having empty boxes shipped to Geneva, Switzerland. The jewelry was delivered to his apartment at Olympic Tower, a few blocks away from the Bulgari store. At the time, Olympic Tower was one of only two buildings in Manhattan that allowed apartments to be owned in the name of untraceable corporations, a form of anonymous wealth. The other such building was Trump Tower. It was not the only time that Trump and Khashoggi would be publicly linked as supposedly very rich men who pinched what would have been pocket change for billionaires.

The grand jury heard testimony regarding 202 instances in which the global jewelry store mailed empty boxes to customers. The patrons had avoided paying a total of $1.5 million in sales taxes. Trump stood out among the customers because he made a deal to testify so that he would not be targeted.

The sales tax scandal posed a much bigger threat to Trump's riches than the accumulated sales tax itself. As the owner of two Atlantic City casinos, any criminal charge would have jeopardized Trump's casino license. Evading more than $5,000 of sales tax in just the two instances the grand jury reviewed could have qualified Trump for a felony indictment. Indeed, if New Jersey casino regulators had wanted to make an issue of his mere involvement in the scheme, even without a formal criminal charge, that might have justified revoking his license. Trump retained Howard Rubenstein, the go-to crisis publicist for rich New Yorkers in trouble, to deal with Bastone and other reporters. Rubenstein said Trump had engaged only in "bona fide transactions"; he had done nothing wrong.

Robert Abrams, who was then the New York state attorney general, did not target Trump or the other buyers. Instead (like the New Jersey gaming regulators who brought the full force of law enforcement down on cocktail waitresses and blackjack dealers), Abrams went after the easy targets. He asked the grand jury to indict a local company manager, as well as Nicola Bulgari, an Italian citizen who was part owner of the store bearing his name. The grand jury granted Abrams's requests, charging the two men with 213 crimes. For a time, Nicola Bulgari was treated as a fugitive because he did not promptly return to New York from Italy. Abrams sought a stay behind bars for the two men.

Shortly before Christmas 1986, Mayor Ed Koch announced that Nicola Bulgari and the store manager had pled guilty, but would not get any prison time. Koch was furious about the light sentences. He also believed that the "prominent persons" who were customers should have faced felony charges.

"We should embarrass them," Koch said. "For a prominent person, even fifteen days in jail is a prominent sentence." Any jail time would have cost Trump his casino license for sure.

In 1987, Khashoggi and Trump again found themselves in the public eye together. Khashoggi had commissioned the construction of a luxurious 281-foot yacht, one of the world's largest, with polished bird's-eye maple paneling and a master suite bathroom that one visitor joked was large enough to land a helicopter in. He named the sleek white vessel *Nabila* in honor of a daughter. The vessel was christened "The Flying Saucer" for the 1983 James Bond blockbuster *Never Say Never Again*.

Khashoggi lost the boat when he could not pay his creditors. In 1987, it went to Trump, who renamed it the *Trump Princess*. (Renaming a boat is considered bad luck, an insight missed by some of his casino competitors and high-rollers.) Along with the boat came the enormous bills to maintain and fuel it. Trump—who, as best I can tell, only traveled once on the ship and complained about being seasick on the overnight voyage from New York to the docks at his Atlantic City marina casino—escaped the $1.7 million in New Jersey sales taxes he would have owed on the boat. He achieved this by purchasing the ship through an offshore corporation he alone owned. He then leased the ship to himself so that he only had to pay sales taxes on the monthly lease payments, just as people who lease cars do. State tax officials looked into the deal, but concluded the tax avoidance was within the law.

In 1990, when Trump's empire was on the verge of collapse because he could not pay back more than three billion borrowed dollars, Trump's allies told *The New York Times* that he was about to sell the yacht for $110 million, more than three times the roughly $30 million he said he had paid for it three years earlier. It was an obviously absurd effort to hype his wealth. The newspaper wryly noted that "the Trump Organization refused to comment publicly," code for not openly supporting a story it had planted through allies. The yacht was then sold—for millions less than Trump said he paid—to Saudi prince Al-Waleed Bin Talal bin Abdulaziz al Saud, who would soon acquire another Trump trophy property, the Plaza Hotel across from Central Park in Manhattan.

Also in 1990, Trump and Khashoggi were again linked through a prank designed to find out who was the cheapest rich person in New York. The satirical magazine *Spy* created a phony business and sent $1.11 refund checks to fifty-eight rich New Yorkers. Those who cashed the checks then got another refund check from the fake firm for half as much money. The prank ended when only two self-proclaimed billionaire penny pinchers were left. Donald Trump and Adnan Khashoggi had the dubious distinction of endorsing and depositing into their bank accounts fake refund checks for thirteen cents each.

15

—

"BETTER THAN HARVARD"

Michael Sexton, a management consultant and for-profit education entrepreneur, wrangled a brief meeting with Donald Trump in 2004. Sexton proposed licensing Trump's name for online real estate courses similar to those periodically required for agents to maintain their licenses. Trump embraced the idea. In fact, Trump liked the idea so much that when Sexton and his associates returned to Trump Tower to close the deal, Trump announced that, rather than licensing his name, Trump was going to own the company. Sexton would get a 5 percent ownership stake and a quarter-million-dollar annual salary to run the operation.

"At Trump University, we teach success," Trump said, looking into the camera in a 2005 promotional video. "That's what it's all about—success. It's going to happen to you. We're going to have professors and adjunct professors that are absolutely terrific—terrific people, terrific brains, successful. We are going to have the best of the best. These are all people that are handpicked by me."

None of those statements were true.

First, there was no "university," neither in the commonly understood sense of the word—as an institution where many branches of advanced learning take place—nor under the laws of New York, which prohibit any enterprise from using the word *university* in its name unless it has been so authorized by the state education department.

Rather than any sort of campus, Trump University headquarters was located in a building at 40 Wall Street, which Trump owns. In July 2016, *Bloomberg Businessweek* magazine reported that 40 Wall Street was also the address of choice for stock market swindlers, boiler room operators, and penny stock cons. According to the public alert list, which is issued by the federal Securities and Exchange Commission to warn people away from scams, no other address hosts as many unregistered stock brokerage firms.

One week after Trump University declared itself, New York officials ordered Trump to stop using the word *university*. Trump and Sexton basically ignored these demands for five years, though in 2010 they did change the name to the Trump Entrepreneur Initiative. Trump testified that he knew next to nothing about that, and referred questions to Sexton.

The faux university also did not have professors, not even part-time adjunct professors, and the "faculty" (as they were called) were certainly not "the best of the best." They were commissioned sales people, many with no experience in real estate. One managed a fast food joint, as Senator Marco Rubio would point out during the March 3 Republican primary debate in 2016. Two other instructors were in personal bankruptcy while collecting fees from would-be Trump University graduates eager to learn how to get rich.

Trump did not even honor his commitment to handpick the faculty. In 2012, when Trump was sued for civil fraud in California, attorney Rachel Jensen read the names of one faculty member after another, displayed photographs of them, and offered video footage of faculty at Trump University "live events." Trump, who complained that this line of questioning was a waste of time, could not identify a single person. "Too many years ago . . . too many years ago . . . it's ancient history," he said. Some of these events had taken place fewer than two years earlier. Again and again and again, Trump testified that he could not remember.

It is worth noting that Trump's memory seemed quite keen three years later, in 2001, when he insisted that he had watched on television as thousands of Muslims in New Jersey cheered while the Twin Towers burned. No videotape, photograph, or police report has ever been found to support this memory. But Trump maintains his memory was correct. After all, as he told a 2015 campaign audience in Iowa, he is possessed of "the world's greatest memory."

In any event, when Jensen finally asked if Trump could name for her "one good live events instructor" for Trump University, Trump replied, "I don't know the instructors," thereby completely contradicting his promise that he would handpick them all.

Trump made another odd promise in the Trump University promotional video: "We're going to teach you better than the business schools are going to teach you, and I went to the best business school," he said. "We're going to teach you better. I think it's going to be a better education and it's going to teach you what you need to know."

None of this was true either. The only thing close to being true was that he went to "the best business school." Trump never attended the noted Wharton School at Penn, but he did enroll for two years in a four-year undergraduate program.

Based on the testimony Trump gave Rachel Jensen in 2012, it's ludicrous to argue that Trump University offered a better education than any top business school. Trump himself acknowledged that Sexton, whom he'd put in charge of running Trump University, "didn't have much of a background in real estate." Trump also said he didn't remember whether Sexton had ever run a school before. "It's too long ago," he said.

Trump also denied knowing how much a three-day seminar cost. "It was a long time ago," he testified. "I don't know."

When Jensen asked whether "someone who had no experience buying or selling real estate" should be "qualified to charge tens of thousands of dollars for a three-day real estate mentorship," Trump replied, "I really—I really can't answer . . . I don't know what his background is. I really don't know. Maybe he's a super genius in so many ways. I don't know. I mean, I can't tell you. I just can't tell you that."

Trump also admitted that he had never reviewed the scripts that were provided to the live events instructors: "I don't believe so, no," he testified. Clearly, Trump could not vouch for the value of the lectures, which both government investigators and students seeking refunds described as scripts of polished high-pressure sales tactics of little to no educational value.

The testimony above all comes from a 2012 suit, but two other lawsuits claimed that the whole Trump University enterprise was a fraud—a scam in which the desperate and the gullible paid Trump about $40 million for what turned out to be high-pressure salesmanship. In a 2013 case, New York Attorney General Eric Schneiderman said the three-day Trump University seminar (which cost $1,497) promised access to a special "database" of lenders. What it actually offered was a list that traced back to the *Scotsman Guide,* a monthly magazine I accessed for free on the Internet.

New York was not the only state where authorities suspected Trump University was a con. In Texas, undercover state consumer fraud agents attended many of the fifty-seven free Trump University seminars held over seven months. They later compiled a report.

Among the investigators' findings was that students who attended a "next level" seminar "are taught to prey upon homeowners in financial turmoil and to target foreclosure properties." They were also instructed, on the first morning of the three-day course, "to call their credit card companies, banks, and mortgage companies and ask for an increase or extension of credit so that they may finance the 'Gold Elite' package purchase. Defendant Trump U will even ask attendees to call their bank during these one-on-one sessions while the representative waits. The primary goal of the 3-day seminars appears to be more high pressure sales tactics in an attempt to induce them into purchasing Defendant Trump U's 'Gold Elite' package for $35,000."

The consumer protection investigators also reported that what Trump University taught "is out of date, inapplicable to the Texas real estate market, and generally of little practical value. Moreover, the so-called strategies that are taught are highly speculative and may be tantamount to encouraging attendees to sell real estate without a license, which is illegal in Texas."

The state report also said the sales agents posing as faculty "falsely assert at these 'free workshops' that the classes are approved continuing education credit for realtors," even though they were not approved. Finally, calling the operation a university violated a Texas law similar to the one in New York. Trump University had not even obtained a required Texas license and had not registered to pay sales tax, as mandated by state law. (Sexton later testified that the taxes were eventually paid.)

To the seasoned fraud investigators who compiled the report, the case against Trump seemed ironclad. The investigators concluded with the suggestion that Trump—who, to solicit customers, signed letters that said, "I can turn anyone into a successful real estate investor, including you"—be named personally in a civil action suit alleging deceptive trade practices.

We know all this because John Owens, who retired in 2011 as chief deputy in the Texas attorney general's consumer protection unit, made the internal report public in 2016. The Texas attorney general's office, Owens's former employer, responded with a letter citing six laws Owens may have broken in releasing the report and suggesting his law license might be revoked.

The documents Owens released included an analysis of the defenses Trump could be expected to argue if the matter went to court and why the staff felt he would lose. Owens also released a January 2010 letter signed by Rick Berlin, an assistant Texas attorney general, proposing that the state demand restitution for the Texans who felt swindled, as well as further penalties for deceptive and illegal conduct. In all, Berlin recommended demanding $5.4 million and a permanent order banning Trump and his fake university from ever doing business in Texas again.

Greg Abbott, the Texas attorney general, took no public action.

After Owens made the internal report public, state officials put their own spin on the decision not to demand restitution or file a public action. They insisted that Abbott had actually scored a win for Texas by not following his staff's advice. Abbott has since been elected governor. He endorsed Trump in 2016. Abbott's office said he had done his job in forcing what it characterized as a bad business to leave Texas.

Abbott has not explained the reasons he would endorse for president someone who ran a business so crooked he ran it out of the state. It could not be determined whether Trump moved on under threat of action by Abbott or simply because he decided the Texas market for Trump University's offerings had been exhausted. No documentation was provided to either effect.

In 2013, three years after Berlin failed to persuade Abbott to adopt his recommendation to recover money for Texas consumers, Trump donated $35,000 to Abbott's campaign for governor. A much shorter time period between campaign gift and official inaction occurred in Florida.

On September 13 of the same year, Florida's attorney general, Pam Bondi, announced that her office was considering joining the New York attorney general in investigating Trump University as a possible fraud. That week, a $25,000 check from the Donald J. Trump Foundation was delivered to Attorney General Pam Bondi's reelection campaign organization, And Justice for All. Ivanka Trump also sent a personal check donating $500 to support Bondi's reelection. On September 17, Bondi announced that her office would not join the New York fraud investigation, citing a lack of evidence and claiming her office had received only a single complaint.

Both Bondi (a lawyer) and Trump would have known that many would consider it improper for an attorney general to accept campaign money from the subject of a possible fraud investigation. In fact, on the last day of June 2016, Trump himself denounced Loretta Lynch, the attorney general of the United States, for having a half-hour conversation with former president Bill Clinton during a chance encounter on the Phoenix Airport tarmac. The two should not have spoken at all, Trump said, because the Federal Bureau of Investigation was still probing Hillary Clinton's use of a private email server when she was secretary of state.

"Who would do this?" Trump demanded. "I just think it's so terrible, I think it's so horrible."

Trump pointed out that he was campaigning against a rigged system. The Phoenix meeting was "evidence of a rigged system," he said. He made no comment about his own investigation in Florida or his substantial campaign donation to Bondi.

Contrary to Bondi's claim, there had been more than one Florida complaint about Trump's education business. When reporter Scott Maxwell asked the Florida attorney general's office for all records of complaints regarding Trump's education enterprises in 2013, he received 8,491 pages of records. The documents showed that Bondi, like Bill McCollum, her predecessor, had turned away many pleas for help. Citizens, some of them quite elderly, were told to complain to some other government agency or file a lawsuit on their own. One man said the $26,000 he paid for a Trump education drove him into bankruptcy. There were also complaints that there was no practical way to get a refund because the Trump offices in Boca Raton had closed.

Trump's Florida operation was run by Michael and Irene Millin. The Millins had done quite well for themselves; like Donald Trump, they were once featured on the syndicated television show *Lifestyles of the Rich and Famous*. They were also a couple well known to fraud investigators across the country as marketers of get rich quick schemes. They were the subject of complaints about offices that closed suddenly, leaving employees and suppliers unpaid. Their pricey seminars claiming people could borrow vast sums at no interest and qualify for big government grants drew action by attorneys general in thirty-four states. Among them was none other than Greg Abbott when he was the top law enforcement official in Texas.

Why Trump would associate with the Millins is a question thus far unasked during presidential debates and campaign events, though learning about the couple's dubious record in business would not have required a lengthy or expensive background investigation. A simple Internet search would have done the trick.

Furthermore, Congress prohibits charities, including Trump's private foundation, from making any political contributions like the one he made to Bondi's campaign. For both Trump and Bondi, the cashing of that check opens the prospect of prosecution for felonies. In June 2016, a Boston lawyer named Whitfield Larrabee asked federal prosecutors to seek indictments of Bondi and Trump for bribery. "If it looks like a bribe and quacks like a bribe, I think it's a bribe," Larrabee said.

The explanation offered by Trump's foundation will likely induce utter disbelief from people who run charitable foundations or who work in their grant-making departments. It will also raise the eyebrows of any experienced public corruption prosecutor. Grant-making foundations are required to disclose the names of their recipients in an annual report to the IRS known as Form 990. That document is signed, just like your personal income tax return, under penalty of perjury.

The Trump Foundation Form 990 for 2013 makes no mention of a donation to Bondi's campaign arm, And Justice for All. However, it does show a $25,000 gift to a charity with a slightly different name, Justice for All, located in Wichita, Kansas. That organization, whose charitable mission is training anti-abortion organizers, said it did not receive a penny from Trump's foundation.

Allen Weisselberg, who is both the Trump Organization chief financial officer and treasurer of Donald Trump's charitable foundation, blamed the failure to properly report the gift on a typographical error—a heavy burden for a mistyped letter or two to bear, especially when it turned out that the actual $25,000 check was made out to a group with the same name as the Bondi campaign, this one with a Utah address. The Utah charity had not gotten any Trump money, either.

According to Weisselberg, the same staff work on Trump's business and his foundation. He told *The Washington Post* that an unnamed clerk received a request for payment from Bondi's organization, And Justice for All. If true, that means Bondi solicited Trump when he and his faux educational organization were under investigation for fraud.

Even more astonishing was the statement And Justice for All treasurer Nancy Watkins made to the *Tampa Bay Times* in 2013. She said Bondi's campaign was "comfortable with the propriety of the contribution from the Trump Foundation."

While no one involved felt anything was wrong in Florida, Trump had a very different view of what happened in a federal court case in California, where people sued him and Trump University as a fraud.

His answers to lawyer Jensen's questions were made public at the request of numerous news organizations. Those requests were filed with Judge Gonzalo Curiel, the federal judge overseeing two of the fraud cases in San Diego. The day that Judge Curiel made the testimony available, Trump went on the attack.

"I have a judge who is a hater of Donald Trump, a hater . . . he is not doing the right thing," Trump said, inadvertently sparking a debate over whether he would respect the independence of the judiciary as president. Trump made no mention of the judge's decision to make some of the material in the fraud case public, a dot that many news reports did not connect. Trump instead suggested an investigation of "the judge, who happens to be Mexican." Judge Curiel, a former federal prosecutor, was born in Indiana and graduated from law school there.

The next day, Trump continued his attack on the judge's heritage. "I'm building the wall, I'm building the wall," Trump said of his proposed barrier between the United States and Mexico. "I have a Mexican judge. He's of Mexican heritage. He should have recused himself, not only for that, for other things."

The comments prompted the *National Review*, an influential conservative political magazine that opposes Trump, to mock him: "It turns out that Donald Trump's legal philosophy, such as it is, is like his philosophy of everything else: Donald Trump likes judges who like Donald Trump."

As of July 2016, Trump has sought to keep the public from seeing the rest of the court record requested by news organizations, especially the video of lawyer Jensen questioning him under oath. Simultaneously, he derides the fraud allegations as nonsense and declares that he was winning in all three court cases. Yet he fears the video of his deposition. Trump's lawyers have argued that releasing the video of his testimony "serves no legitimate purpose in the litigation and will only taint" future jurors should the case go to trial. Release of the video would cause "extreme prejudice" that will "imperil" Trump's right to a fair civil trial. "This Court should not let the judicial process be abused in this way."

Meanwhile, Trump was embroiled in new problems he'd created for himself and his foundation, problems that put a number of charities helping military veterans at risk of losing their tax-exempt status.

16

—

TRUMP CHARITIES

Liberty House, a small veterans charity in New Hampshire, received a call from the Trump campaign on February 5, 2016, the day before the first primary vote in the nation for the 2016 election. Keith Howard, an Army veteran who runs the charity, said he was asked to come to a Trump rally in Londonderry on Monday, the night before the vote, to accept a $100,000 donation from Trump.

Howard declined. It was not that his veterans support group could not use the money, which was equal to a third of their annual budget. And it was not that they disliked Trump or preferred another candidate, either. Howard declined because it is illegal for charities to participate in partisan politics.

"I told them it would endanger our status as a charitable organization," Howard told me. "I said we couldn't do it."

He was right, but while he passed on the opportunity to lend his charity's name in support of Trump, others did not. The campaign continued to engage charities in ways that helped Trump but that jeopardized the organizations' ability to receive tax-deductible donations, which are strictly regulated by Congress.

Eventually Liberty House did get the promised money, which came not from Trump but from a wealthy resident of Trump Tower.

During another campaign event in Iowa, less than two weeks before the call to Keith Howard, Trump announced a drive to "raise some money for the vets." Trump and his campaign said more than $6 million was raised on the spot, but when journalists from a number of organizations asked which veterans groups could expect to benefit from the fund-raiser, they received no answers.

Four months passed with no evidence that any money had been distributed. Just before *The Washington Post* ran a story about where the money had (or hadn't) gone, Trump had checks sent to veterans groups by overnight delivery. A few days later, he announced he had turned over $5.6 million, including $1 million of his own money, to veterans, and his campaign handed out a list of the recipients.

Trump used the questions about the distributions to lambaste journalists generally, and called one reporter a sleaze.

"The press should be ashamed of themselves," Trump said. Instead of being showered with unqualified praise, Trump complained, he was asked for evidence that the donated money was actually going to veterans charities. He was also asked why the amount raised was about a million and a half less than the $6 million campaign manager Corey Lewandowski had quoted at the time. The response was that not everyone fulfilled his or her pledges, an interesting answer since a charitable pledge is a legally enforceable obligation if made in writing, and it is standard practice for charities to get pledges in writing.

Journalists had good reason to ask where the charity dollars were, given Trump's long history of promising donations and no public record of them actually being made.

For example, Donald Trump often boasts about his education at the University of Pennsylvania. But despite his penchant for putting his name on buildings and flaunting what he says is his immense wealth, there are no buildings bearing the Trump name on the Philadelphia campus. There are no lecture halls, no classrooms, no line of books on a library shelf, not even a chair with the Trump name. His name does not even appear in annual listings of donors that Penn, like nearly all colleges, publishes in brochures and other materials sent to graduates and supporters.

Of course it could be, as Trump himself has said, that he prefers to make donations privately, without his name attached.

When *The Art of the Deal* was published in 1987, Trump publicly promised that all royalties would go to help the homeless, Vietnam veterans, and people with AIDS and multiple sclerosis. The book sold so well—it was a number one *New York Times* bestseller—that Trump said he expected to give away at least $4 million.

Long ago I asked about that. The Trump Organization did not return any of my calls with an answer. Trump has since said that he eventually gave the money to his foundation, though his total gifts to it since its creation (in the same year that the book came out) have come out to less than $2 million.

Then there's his *Monopoly*-like board game. When Trump and executives from Milton-Bradley introduced *Trump: The Game* in 1989, the developer surprised everyone by declaring those royalties would go to charity, too.

Milton-Bradley took Trump at his word. It also figured it might improve sales, which were weak, if people realized their purchases would not enrich a presumed billionaire but go to charity. Its television ads told potential buyers: "Mr. Trump's proceeds from *Trump: The Game* will be donated to charity."

Trump has said he made $808,000 and that the money was donated to his Donald J. Trump Foundation.

A year after the board game was created, Trump made a deal with banks to avoid personal bankruptcy. It included a clause that put him on an allowance. It was a big allowance: $5.4 million per year to support his lifestyle, including a $100,000 limit on gifts to charity in the first year.

At the time, I spent a day calling New York and New Jersey charities trying to find any disclosures of gifts made by Trump. Years earlier, I had created America's first hard news beat covering charities and trained the original *Chronicle of Philanthropy* news staff, so I was in a position to know many people in this sector. But call after call produced nothing. Finally, one professional fund-raiser told me that Trump had been asked to buy a table at a charity dinner and Trump asked for a discount, which was declined.

These days Trump calls himself "an ardent philanthropist," but there is almost no public record that he has made much in the way of charitable gifts, and certainly not gifts in line with his claimed wealth of more than $10 billion. In 2016, reporter David A. Fahrenthold used the same approach I tried a quarter century earlier, calling more than two hundred charities in search of gifts by Trump. He identified only a single personal donation by Trump in the seven years before he became the Republican nominee for president. It was a gift of less than $10,000 reported in 2009 by the New York City Police Athletic League, and it may have been recorded as a personal gift by mistake, Fahrenthold noted.

● ● ●

Trump is not even the largest donor to his own foundation. The family that owns the World Wrestling Federation gave more. Since 2006, the Donald J. Trump Foundation tax filings show only a single gift from its namesake. It was for $30,000. The major donors in recent years have been vendors doing business with Trump; they offer gifts that can reasonably be viewed as a kind of legal kickback by the vendors of Trump ties and other products and services sold with the Trump name.

Having contributions made this way would also be tax-wise if, as reported elsewhere in this book, Trump pays little or no income tax, thanks partly to special rules that allow major real estate holders to report zero income for tax purposes. While charitable gifts are tax-deductible for someone who pays taxes, to anyone with no taxable income, that deduction is worth nothing.

Trump often encourages others to give, especially during his campaign, mixing partisan politics with charity, despite Congress making that an absolute no-no if the charities participate.

The record shows that Trump makes little or no effort to check out the veterans organizations he associates with, just as he has often failed to make even minimal inquiries into some of his business partners and associates.

In September 2015, Trump boycotted one of the Republican primary debates because Megyn Kelly, a Fox News personality, would be the on-air host. Trump instead went to the Battleship Iowa, now a museum at anchor in Long Beach, California, to deliver what his campaign said would be a major address on national defense.

Trump praised the sponsor of the event, Veterans for a Strong America, and told the audience that "hundreds of thousands" of people belonged to the organization. There were evidently two related organizations, both nonprofits, though Trump and his host never made that clear to the audience on the ship or watching on television. One was a charity, the other one of those dark money political groups that have expanded since the Supreme Court's 2010 Citizens United decision, enabling money from undisclosed sources to influence elections.

A quick Internet check would have revealed to the Trump campaign that the IRS had revoked the nonprofit status of Veterans for a Strong America due to their failure to file required disclosure reports. A charity disclosure organization, Guidestar, reported that it had no record of any board of directors. Every indication pointed to Veterans for a Strong America being a one-man enterprise run by a South Dakota lawyer named Joel Arends, whose operation was under investigation for suspected election improprieties in Arizona and Texas. Reporters later learned the organization had thirty dollars in the bank and debts ten times that size. None of this was in line with Trump's promotion of the group's immense size, influence, and good works.

But the nature of much of Trump's declared charitable giving is far from the only illusory aspect of Trump's life. He also has imaginary employees.

17

—

IMAGINARY FRIENDS

After the destruction of the Bonwit Teller building, a chorus of incredulous New Yorkers criticized Trump's decision to destroy the façade art along with it. A front-page *New York Times* story reported unsuccessful attempts to reach Trump. Instead, the paper got a call from "John Baron, a vice president of the Trump Organization." Baron described himself as Donald Trump's spokesperson. He said that taking the sculptures down would have cost $32,000, delayed the construction of Trump Tower by three weeks, and run the risk of killing people if the stones crashed to the ground. As for the missing grillwork, Baron said, "We don't know what happened."

But there was no John Baron. The caller was Donald Trump.

For years, Trump telephoned journalists using the name John Baron (or Barron). He posed as a publicist, planting stories about how this or that woman was in awe of him or how some business deal was about to come his way. It worked on the *Times* reporter who covered the Bonwit Teller destruction because in 1980 it was still possible not to be familiar with Trump's distinctive cadence, speech patterns, and tone. But gossip columnists like Liz Smith knew Trump was planting stories about himself and asking that his words be attributed to the fictional John Baron or master publicist Howard Rubenstein.

The technique lent credibility to stories by tricking journalists (whose behavior Trump has said he studied closely). Five years after deceiving *The New York Times* in the Bonwit scandal, Trump—posing as John Baron—planted the gist of a story about his upstart New Jersey Generals football team. Then, using his own name, Trump confirmed what Baron had said, which got the story published.

The deception began when Barron (spelled with two *R*s this time) told a wire service reporter that the owners of all the United States Football League teams had verbally agreed to pick up part of the cost of the Generals' quarterback. That seemed like an odd form of corporate socialism, not competition. Trump had signed quarterback Doug Flutie to a six-year deal worth $8.25 million, an eye-popping figure at the time. The nascent league played a spring and summer season starting in 1982 in hopes of competing for fans and raking in the kind of money enjoyed by the National Football League during its fall and winter schedule. Owning a sports team in North Jersey also gave Trump opportunities to connect with Garden State politicians (at the same time he was building his first casino on the shore in South Jersey).

Barron identified himself as a Trump Organization vice president, a spokesman for Trump. He said Trump expected the other team owners to honor their verbal commitment to share in the cost of Flutie's huge paycheck. "When a guy goes out and spends more money than a player is worth, he expects to get partial reimbursement from the [other team] owners," Barron said in suspiciously Trumpian language.

Hours later, Trump spoke to the same news service. He confirmed what Barron had said, adding that he had indeed paid too much for Flutie's services, but that the other owners should share in the cost because he spent so much "for the good of the league." The other owners, naturally, had no interest in paying Trump's bills (a subject we will return to later).

For years, Trump planted stories using the name John Baron, including many unsourced items in the gossipy *New York Post*. But he did not limit his use of fake names to self-promotion. He also used his alter ego to menace enemies.

John Szabo, the immigration lawyer representing the unpaid Polish Brigade on the Bonwit Teller demolition job, had filed claims against Trump assets, hoping to prompt payment. If that did not get the workers paid, Szabo knew the liens would protect them in a subsequent lawsuit. One day a man named John Baron called Szabo, demanding that he drop the case.

"Mr. Baron had told me, in the one telephone conversation that I had with him, that Donald Trump was upset because I was ruining his credit reputation by filing the mechanics liens," Mr. Szabo told documentary filmmaker Libby Handros. "And Mr. Trump was thinking of filing a personal lawsuit against me for $100 million for defaming his, uh . . . reputation."

During the 1990 federal court trial before Judge Charles E. Stewart Jr. to enforce payment of the money owed to the Polish Brigade, Trump admitted to using the name John Baron, but said he didn't start doing so until "years later," after the menacing 1980 call Szabo described.

Handros's scathing 1991 film, *Trump: What's the Deal?*, was shown only twice. Because of Trump's litigation threats, no television broadcaster or distributor would risk presenting the film, according to Handros and others on the project at the time. A quarter century later, after Trump launched his 2016 presidential campaign, Handros found that continued fear of Trump lawsuits still made it impossible to get her film shown in public.

But Handros would not bow to intimidation. She posted the movie trailer online. After upwards of a million people people watched it, she updated the opening sequences for to-day's voters. Then Handros put the entire film on YouTube, where a half million people watched the eighty-minute movie. She then made it available for rental or purchase on iTunes, hoping people might organize parties to show friends what Trump did not want them to know.

Trump stopped posing as John Baron after the Polish Bri-gade trial testimony and a screening of the suppressed doc-umentary exposed his alternate identity to some New York journalists. He switched to the name John Miller. This decep-tion also came to light, but that didn't stop him from resur-recting John Miller during the 2016 presidential campaign.

18

—

IMAGINARY LOVERS

The unraveling of Trump's John Miller deception began with an NBC *Today Show* report in late June 1991. The nationally televised morning program said Donald Trump had just dumped his longtime girlfriend, Marla Maples—a curvy blonde the tabloids called "Trump's Georgia Peach"— and taken up with Carla Bruni, a sleek Italian model and singer. The story made the cover of the *New York Post* (a tabloid where Trump often planted items about his business successes), as well as the tabloid *Newsday*.

That major news organizations would report on the romances of a real estate developer is a testament to Trump's success in creating public interest in his life, or at least those aspects he wanted covered: Trump the Modern Midas and Trump the Great Don Juan.

Sue Carswell, a reporter for *People* magazine new on the Trump beat, called the Trump Organization seeking an interview with Trump. Minutes later she got a call back and turned on her tape recorder.

The caller identified himself as John Miller. He said he had just been hired to handle Donald Trump's public relations because The Donald was too busy to return calls himself, given "the important, beautiful women who call him all the time." He listed pop singer Madonna, actress Kim Basinger, and Carla Bruni specifically. For a freshly hired Trump publicist, Miller seemed exceptionally informed about his boss. He gave lengthy, detailed, and nuanced observations on Trump's emotional state, his relationships with various women, and his eagerness to marry again.

Refuting the *Newsday* report that Trump had left his wife Ivana for his longtime mistress, Miller said that Trump "didn't leave for Marla. He really left for himself. He didn't leave for Marla. He never left for Marla. He was going to leave anyway. Marla was there, but he was going to leave anyway. So now he has somebody named Carla who is beautiful . . . Carla is a very beautiful woman from Italy whose father is one of the wealthiest men in Europe."

Carswell asked for the name of the father. "Her father's name is . . ." Miller paused, evidently realizing he didn't know the father's name. "Her name is Carla Bruni Fredesh," he said. "I don't know how to spell the last name." It was spelled Tedeschi. The father Trump referred to (Alberto Bruni Tedeschi) is a classical music composer and scion of an old industrial family; Carla Bruni's mother is a concert pianist.

Miller told Carswell that Bruni had a fling with guitarist Eric Clapton before starting "a big thing" with Mick Jagger, "and then she dropped Mick Jagger for Donald, and that's where it is right now. And again he's not making any commitments to Carla, just so you understand."

Bruni later said that Trump had indeed called her a few days before the *People* interview. She told Trump that her sister would be joining her in New York, and—according to author Harry Hurt III, in his book *Lost Tycoon*—Trump offered Bruni and her sister a room gratis at his Plaza Hotel across from Central Park. Bruni accepted the offer, even though, as she later said, she had no interest in a liaison with a man she referred to as "the King of Tacky."

"He's living with Marla and he's got three other girlfriends," Miller continued, describing an intense competition to become the second Mrs. Donald J. Trump. "When he makes the decision, that will be a very lucky woman . . . competitively, it's tough. It was for Marla and it will be for Carla."

Carswell was not fooled. She knew almost immediately that John Miller was actually Trump. But before writing her account, Carswell played her tape recording for gossip columnist Cindy Adams. "That's Donald," Adams said.

Carswell's *People* magazine story began in a most unusual way: "There are interesting stories, there are moving stories, and there are funny stories. And there are stories that are simply bizarre."

After hearing the tape, Maples told *People* she was "shocked and devastated . . . I feel betrayed at the deepest level." She added that she doubted Trump was with Bruni. "I think he's making this whole thing up to get a playboy image," she said.

Just days earlier, Maples had accompanied Trump to his birthday party in Atlantic City. She had been kept out of sight for years. Sometimes she appeared at public events, but always with a beard (a man posing as her boyfriend) to throw off suspicion that she and Trump were having an affair. This was to be a triumphant night for a long-suffering mistress, her first public event with Trump as a couple, even though he was still married to Ivana.

On their way to the event, two miles away at the Trump Taj Mahal casino, Maples and Trump argued over whether his shirt was appropriately formal. They appeared happy at the party, but things must have devolved thereafter. The next morning, the doors to their twenty-sixth-floor suite at Trump's Castle were off the hinges. Tom Fitzsimmons, a former boyfriend who often accompanied Maples to Trump events and who had come to accompany them to the airfield for the trip back to New York, found Maples in tears and Trump about to walk out the broken doorway. After Hurt reported the incident, I checked with my own sources, who confirmed the fight and said there had been other arguments that left physical evidence.

Just days after the Taj birthday party, NBC's *Today Show* and the tabloids reported—without identifying their sources—that Trump had had it with Maples and had taken up with Carla Bruni. That set in motion the events that ended two weeks later (July 8, 1991) with *People* magazine outing Trump as John Miller. Carswell had caught "Donald Trump posing as a fictitious PR man" for himself. Soon after the article came out, Trump called Carswell and fessed up.

Three months later, Marla Maples appeared on *Designing Women*, a long-running CBS sitcom that often used humor to explore serious topics, in an episode called "Marriage Most Foul." The plot was about men who were dishonest in business, two-timed their women, and were underendowed. Maples appeared on screen as herself, and the show's regular characters asked her a series of obvious questions. One was whether it was true, what Maples was quoted as saying in the *New York*

Post. On February 16, 1990, Trump's grinning face filled the *Post* cover next to what Maples had supposedly told her real-life girlfriends: "Best Sex I Ever Had." Not true and never said it, Maples answered, looking directly into the camera as the actresses discussed in mock shock that a newspaper would ballyhoo a made-up story. *Designing Women* being entertainment, not journalism, it may be that Maples was just kidding.

The episode ended with actress Dixie Carter's character phoning Trump: "Hello? Mr. Trump? I hope I'm not disturbing you. I'm just calling you to say—on behalf of the American public—Mr. Trump, we no longer care *who* you date, we really don't. You are no longer obligated to alert the news media every time your pants are on fire because *we don't care.*"

More than two years after that episode aired, the competition to pick the next Mrs. Donald J. Trump ended. The winner was Marla Maples, the long-suffering mistress Trump had publicly humiliated more than once, and the only woman on John Miller's list who had actually slept with Trump. Two months before the wedding, she gave birth to Trump's second daughter, whose future breast size Trump would speculate about on national television before the baby was a year old.

Years later, Trump was handed an opportunity to clear up the matter. Instead, he revived the myth that he had had an affair with Bruni. It happened during one of Trump's many guest appearances on Howard Stern's radio show. Stern, his cohosts, and his guests engage in crude sexual banter, try to encourage women guests to show their breasts, and debate whether they are aroused or turned off by various women in the news.

In 2008, soon after French president Nikolai Sarkozy left

his wife to marry Carla Bruni, making her first lady of France, Stern asked Trump on-air about why he was no longer with Bruni. Instead of acknowledging that they had never been together, Trump replied that Bruni was a "very flat-chested woman, not your kind of woman, Howard." Trump disparaged Bruni's bra size as "smaller than A cup—minus A."

Stern asked if it was true that Bruni had broken up his romance with Marla Maples. "Not true," Trump responded.

Stern pressed. "Did you date her?"

"May I say no comment," Trump said, laughing.

Stern pressed further. "Did you date her?"

"Can I say no comment? Let me just say no comment, I'm trying to be a diplomat for this country. As a great diplomat, Howard, as a great diplomat for this country, let me just say no comment."

"I don't understand something," Stern said, referring to a photo he was eyeing of Bruni in a bikini. Stern called her "magnificent" and asked Trump, "Is she not that hot?"

"Well, let's say that there are better . . . there are better by large margins," Trump said.

Stern continued, "Why would Donald Trump stop banging Carla Bruni? She looks magnificent in this picture."

"Well, you stop her, when you meet somebody better . . . it's a complicated thing. But I know Carla, and, um, but I just don't want to comment . . ."

"Was she bad in bed?" Stern asked.

"I can't comment on that," Trump said.

Stern asked why, giving Trump a perfect opportunity to come clean and be diplomatic at the same time. Instead, Trump said, "She's gonna marry the president of France. I want to have good relationships with France, right. I don't want to be criticizing the first lady of France."

When Stern suggested this might have to do with Trump planning to erect some building in France, Trump, as he often does in interviews, picked up what the interviewer said and suggested that it had some truth to it.

Stern continued to ask what it was like to have sex with Bruni.

"I know her, I know her well," Trump said, again implying they had been lovers, "but I can't comment on that 'cause I want to have good relationships with the wonderful country of France."

Trump never told the simple truth that he had never done more than talk to Bruni. He did not disclose that she had denounced him to his face, as Hurt and others reported, for planting stories about their nonexistent relationship.

"Trump is obviously a lunatic," Bruni told the *Daily Mail*, a London newspaper, a few months later. "It's so untrue and I'm deeply embarrassed by it all."

The reasons Trump was not forthright and candid are, ultimately, known only to Trump. But the *Howard Stern Show* was not his last opportunity to come clean about his use of fake identities to create the impression that the world's most desirable women were banging on his bedroom door. The next time he was presented with a chance to set the record straight, Trump chose to tell a whopper on national television. This time, it served a very specific purpose: to advance his pursuit of the Oval Office.

19

—

MYTH MAINTENANCE

Donald Trump relies on two core strategies to manage the public image he has spent decades creating, polishing, and selling.

In the first, he exploits a common weakness of news reporting: the recitation of "facts" without analysis of that which goes unsaid. Trump often threatens to sue journalists, ensuring caution from publishers and broadcasters who want to avoid a costly lawsuit—even one Trump cannot win. This tends to discourage investigation beyond the official talking points.

Trump spent two years suing author Tim O'Brien and his publisher for writing that his net worth was probably not in the billions, but rather the hundreds of millions. After a court dismissed the case, Trump made it clear that he merely wanted to harass O'Brien, not necessarily win damages. "I spent a couple of bucks on legal fees and they spent a whole lot more. I did it to make his life miserable, which I'm happy about,"

Trump bragged. It was a comment that fit cozily within his philosophy of revenge.

In his second core strategy, Trump distorts information, contradicts himself, and blocks inquiries into his conduct by journalists, law enforcement, business regulators, and other people's lawyers. Again, the record shows decades of Trump's skill in pursuing this strategy successfully.

Trump put both strategies to work in the days after he became the presumptive Republican nominee for president, after his last two primary opponents, Ted Cruz and John Kasich, dropped out in early May 2016.

On a Friday morning, Trump called NBC's *Today Show*. A quarter century earlier, *Today* had reported Trump's imagined affair with Carla Bruni as fact, based on a story that Trump himself had planted under a different name. With Trump as the presumptive nominee, that tactic was back in the news. The day before the *Today Show* call, *The Washington Post* had published a story about Trump posing as men named John Baron and John Miller. On its website, the newspaper posted a 1991 tape recording of Miller speaking to *People* magazine's Sue Carswell.

"Is it you [on the tape]?" *Today* host Savannah Guthrie asked.

"No, I don't know anything about it. You're telling me about it for the first time," Trump answered.

Neither aspect of that response was true.

First, Trump had long since confirmed to *People* magazine that he had been posing as John Miller when he planted the Bruni story. Second, even if the accusation were false, it was simply not credible that Trump was hearing about the existence of the tape for the first time from Guthrie. In fact, *The*

Washington Post had asked him about it before publishing its story the day before. Other news organizations were all over it immediately.

Trump carefully follows news about himself, sometimes even recognizing the bylines of reporters in distant cities. When John Rebchook of the *Rocky Mountain News* introduced himself to Trump after his 2005 Colorado speech recommending revenge as a core business strategy, for example, Trump praised some of Rebchook's past articles about proposed Trump developments in Denver. *The Washington Post*'s article about planted news was not news to Trump.

After his false statement to Guthrie, Trump continued: "It doesn't sound like my voice at all. I have many, many people that are trying to imitate my voice and you can imagine that. And this sounds like one of the scams, one of the many scams."

Guthrie did not pursue what Trump meant about "many scams." Instead, she asked whether using a fake name "is something you did rather routinely, that you would call reporters and plant stories and say either you were John Miller or John Baron, but in fact it was actually you on the phone. Is that something you did with any regularity?"

"*No,* and it was not me on the phone—it was not me on the phone. And it doesn't sound like me on the phone, I will tell you that, and it was not me on the phone," Trump said.

Hours later, Katrina Pierson, a Trump campaign spokesperson, appeared on CNN. "It sounds like a great impersonation," Pierson said, "but it's definitely not Mr. Trump."

This particular deception fits into the long pattern of the way Trump conducts himself. He even revealed part of the purpose when speaking to Guthrie, though she did not catch on, as we are about to see.

• • •

Some people argue with the question posed to them, as Bill Clinton infamously did when he said under oath: "It depends on what your definition of is *is*." Others veer off on verbal tangents, hoping to steer the conversation in another direction. Some celebrities arrange to talk to the cameras outside a hearing room just as the main witness against them is about to speak. Some say they need to check their records before answering. And many people use the one catchall that usually cannot be disproved: *I don't recall*. That last option would seem unavailable to Trump, since he declared in October that he enjoys "the world's greatest memory."

Trump's emphatic *Today Show* denials left no escape hatch. There was no equivocation, no request for time to check the record, no hint of faded memory. His flat-out denials contradicted what *People* magazine published in 1991, as well as his 1990 Polish Brigade trial testimony, where, when asked about posing as John Baron, Trump testified, "I believe I used that name on occasion."

So what would prompt Trump to deny the allegation on the *Today Show* call? Surely he must have realized that he'd be caught. This was not like his 2008 comments to Howard Stern, whose audience demographics do not encompass the typical fact-checker. Trump lied to Guthrie while on the cusp of becoming the GOP nominee for president, when his every public word would be captured and closely scrutinized.

A classic public relations strategy is to confront damaging information by getting it out fully and fast so you can put it behind you. To this end, defense lawyers often leak damaging information about their clients to reporters months before a jury will hear the case, sowing uncertainty about guilt in the prospective jury pool in the meantime.

The success of Trump's strategy was illustrated that very

day on *CBS Evening News* with Scott Pelley. "Some mysterious audio tapes surfaced today," the anchor said, playing the snippet about Trump living with Marla Maples and keeping three women on the side. "Is that Donald Trump pretending to be someone else?" While CBS reporter Chip Reid noted that Trump had acknowledged being John Miller in 1991, Pelley did Trump the favor of converting a matter of clear fact into a matter fraught with doubt. Turning hard fact into *who knows?* is one of the most effective strategies for blunting bad news, as public relations executives have advised clients for decades.

On the *Today Show*, Trump employed another of his strategies for deflecting inquiry into his past, chastising Guthrie for even asking about the tape recording. "And when was this, twenty-five years ago?" Trump said. This is where Guthrie did not grasp what Trump was up to. "You mean you are going so low as to talk about something that took place twenty-five years ago about whether I made a phone call . . . Let's get on to more current subjects."

Trump does not want reporters telling people, especially voters, about anything in his past that does not add a sheen to his marketing image. On the campaign trail, Trump dismisses questions about his past as beneath the dignity of journalists, even as he raises decades-old issues about the conduct of his Democratic opponent's husband.

A few weeks before the *Today Show* call, Trump called me at home. He said my questions about his seeking leniency for the drug trafficker who managed his helicopters were so outdated that he didn't remember anything. He then threatened to sue me if he didn't like what I wrote.

Together, these strategies—muddying the facts and deflecting inquiries into past conduct—help ensure that Trump's carefully crafted public persona will not be unmade. He will not suffer the curtain to be pulled back to reveal a man who tricked society into thinking he was all wise and all powerful.

Trump's comments to Guthrie also raise another question: who gave *The Washington Post* that 1991 tape recording? The newspaper said a condition of obtaining the tape was promising never to reveal its source.

Sue Carswell, the only other voice on the tape, told Fox's Megyn Kelly that Trump had to be the source. Had Carswell wanted to make news, she could have sold a piece with her byline about the 1991 interview and Trump's subsequent confession that he was Miller. Kelly asked Carswell what explanation Trump had offered her in his confession that he was John Miller. "He had no explanation," Carswell said. "He just moved the conversations along." She added that Trump then proposed that he, herself, Maples, and a *People* editor go out, which they did.

That Trump might put out a tape and then deny his own voice may seem beyond belief to many people, or at least like something a reporter could benefit from making up. But it makes perfect sense to journalists who are accustomed to publicists dishing on clients or defense lawyers revealing troubling information about defendants. That's the strategy: get bad news out, muddle it, and hope people do not get a clear appreciation of the facts.

One more telling detail shows that Trump was not honest when he spoke to Guthrie on the *Today Show*. *The Washington Post* explicitly asked Trump about the John Miller episode just before publishing its report. "The phone went silent, then dead," the newspaper reported. "When the reporters called back and reached Trump's secretary, she said, 'I heard you got disconnected. He can't take the call now. I don't know what happened.'"

Trump has stymied many journalists (and some law enforcement investigations) in his career, but sowing doubt and threatening litigation are not his only strategies to manage his image and puff up his credentials. Trump has also accepted awards—many awards—that he gave to himself, with help from a friend with a criminal past.

20

—

COLLECTING HONORS

Trump International Golf Links, a breathtaking seaside course in Aberdeen, Scotland, advertises itself as "the world's greatest golf course." That boastful description does not come from Trump. Not exactly, anyway. When the links opened on the treeless dunes in 2013, the American Academy of Hospitality Sciences bestowed the honor in a ceremony near a windswept tee. Trump, wearing a red baseball cap, khakis, and a windbreaker, grinned as he posed with academy president Joseph Cinque, who wore a blue suit for the occasion. The two men held aloft a gaudy, gold-colored plaque declaring that the Trump links was the only golf course in the sport's country of origin to be awarded the coveted Six Star Diamond Award.

The American Academy of Hospitality Sciences holds its honors in very high esteem, calling its Star Diamond awards "the most prestigious emblem of achievement and true quality in the world today." At the 2014 Mar-a-Lago New Year's Eve party, Cinque presented Trump with the academy's lifetime achievement award, evidently the only time the academy has selected someone for this distinction. In all, the Academy has bestowed at least nineteen of its five- and six-star Diamond Awards on Trump golf courses, Trump Tower, a Trump restaurant, the Trump Taj Mahal casino hotel, and Trump's Mar-a-Lago resort in Florida. Citing them as stamps of the finest quality, Trump uses these "very prestigious, coveted" awards to encourage people to spend their money at his resorts.

But these awards are not nearly as hard to win as even a single star in the Michelin guides or a strong rating from Zagat. Michelin, the French tire company, employs teams of undercover restaurant inspectors whose identity is concealed even from top company executives. Michelin awards are so highly coveted that chefs who manage to attain three stars are said to have contemplated suicide at the prospect of being reduced to just two. One star alone can result in a restaurant booking all its tables months in advance. The American Zagat guides, meanwhile, gather the impressions of thousands of diners to evaluate the quality of restaurants, hotels, cabarets, and even golf courses.

The American Academy of Hospitality Services employs neither secret hospitality investigators nor popular opinion. Instead, the American Academy of Hospitality Services awards are chosen, according to the academy itself, by its board of trustees. For years, those trustees included none other than Donald J. Trump, who held the title "Ambassador Extraordinaire." Trump's distinctive signature appears on the academy's plaques alongside that of president Joseph Cinque. In Aberdeen, Trump was accepting an award from a board on which he was a member.

The ties between Trump's organization and the academy

that finds his properties and his person so worthy of accolades run deep. A majority of the trustees bestowing these awards on Trump and his properties were Trump's employees, friends, or retainers. Recent trustees include Ivanka, Trump's oldest daughter, and his son Donald Jr. There's also the chief operating officer of the Trump Organization, Matthew Calamari, and the general manager of Trump's golf course in Bedminster, New Jersey—which itself received a five star Diamond Award from the academy.

Another trustee was Anthony Senecal, Trump's longtime butler and recent historian at Mar-a-Lago, who posted on his Facebook page in 2016 that "pus headed" President Obama "should be hung for treason" and that President Trump would "put an end to the corruption in government !!!" Senecal, decked out in formal butler attire, including a bowler hat, proudly posed for a picture pointing his umbrella at one of the Diamond Awards given to the Florida resort at which he works.

In his role as ambassador extraordinaire, Trump also bestowed awards. With Cinque at his side, Trump gave Knicks basketball forward Amar'e Stoudemire a framed, gold-looking plaque in the Oak Room of the Plaza Hotel in 2010. The award bore the engraved signatures of both Trump and Cinque. In a 2009 video tribute, Trump praised Cinque, saying, "There's nobody like him—he's a special guy." The year before that, Cinque was one of the judges at the Trump-owned Miss Universe pageant.

Beyond having a board stacked with trustees that no one could call objective, another unusual aspect of the American Academy of Hospitality Sciences is its president's career in the hospitality industry. He has none.

• • •

Cinque is known by other names. One is "Joey No Socks." Another is "The Preppy Don." If those sound like names that might be associated with a figure involved in organized crime, it's because they are. New York police with a search warrant knocked on the door of Cinque's Park Avenue South apartment in 1989. Cinque declined to let them in. The police applied a battering ram. Inside the apartment they found a trove of stolen art, including two Marc Chagall prints valued at $40,000. They had been taken in an art gallery heist. Cinque made a deal to plead to a misdemeanor, but prosecutors scrapped the plea bargain after Cinque was seen talking to John Gotti, the "dapper don" who became head of the Gambino crime family by arranging the murder of his predecessor, Paul Castellano—one of the secret owners of the company that supplied concrete for many Trump buildings.

Gotti told Cinque that he would "take care of the DA," an apparent reference to Anne Heyman, the prosecutor who had offered the plea bargain. Writer John Connolly, a former New York City police detective who wrote many revealing articles about Trump, mobsters, and corruption in high places, broke this story in *New York Magazine* in 1995.

Heyman ordered a more thorough investigation of Cinque. She alleged that the investigation showed that Cinque "was dealing drugs out of his apartment and fencing stolen artwork." Heyman also said that Cinque's apartment on Central Park South appeared to be a retail outlet for stolen clothing, including Armani suits and silk shirts. In 1990, Cinque pleaded guilty to a felony: receiving stolen property.

Cinque described himself very differently in an interview with Connolly, an interview in which he channeled Trump. He bragged about his prowess with women and described his rich new friends. Cinque admitted that he had associated with "the wise guys" in his salad days in what he called "the whole-sale used-car business," but said he gave that up after he took three bullets as the victim of a robbery. Cinque lifted his shirt to show off his scars. The police suspected the scars came from a failed mob hit. Cinque said that experience changed his life. He decided to go uptown and hang out with "Muffy, Buffy, and Biff . . . These trust-fund preppies need someone like me to keep them out of trouble." Hence the moniker "The Preppy Don."

In addition to whatever stolen goods fencing or drug deal-ing Cinque may have been involved with in Manhattan, he established a Midwest connection when he became executive director of the American Academy of Restaurant & Hospital-ity Sciences in Milwaukee around 1985. The group described its honors as "the Academy Awards of the Restaurant Indus-try." A number of well-known restaurants declined to hang these honors on their walls, especially after word got around that the way to get an award might just involve a $1,000-dollar initiation fee and annual dues of $495. Later, the headquarters moved to Cinque's Central Park South apartment, rebranded as the American Academy of Hospitality Sciences.

After Trump announced his campaign for president, ques-tions about his association with Cinque arose again. Cinque declined to accept calls from reporters. The academy's lawyer threatened to sue anyone who made mention of Cinque's criminal history.

Trump employed a different tactic. He told the Associated Press that he hardly knows Cinque. They have posed together many times in many places. The former "Joey No Socks" says he's attended Trump's Mar-a-Lago New Year's Eve party in Palm Beach fourteen years in a row. And what of the fact that Trump was listed on the academy website as "Ambassa-dor Extraordinaire" and trustee just weeks before announcing his presidential bid? Trump said it was meaningless, that he had never attended a board meeting. As for his children and employees being trustees, Trump said, "I don't know that anybody goes." After reporter Hunter Walker of *Yahoo News* asked about that connection, the academy took down that portion of its website.

And what about all those awards? Does Trump have any concerns that his signature is engraved next to that of a convicted felon? What standards does Trump apply in accepting awards, especially considering renowned Manhattan restaurants like Le Cirque and Le Bernardin decline to put the plaques on their walls?

"If a guy's going to give you an award, you take it," Trump said. As for Cinque's criminal history, he said, "You don't tend to look up his whole life story."

"Joey No Socks" was not the only man with a criminal past and shady business practices with whom Trump associated himself again and again in the years just before his 2016 run for the White House. There was also a convicted stock swindler who once served time in prison for driving the stem of a margarita glass into the face of another man in a Lower Manhattan bar.

21

WHO'S THAT?

oments after Donald Trump delivered his profanity-laced remarks on the virtues of revenge in Loveland, Colorado, in 2005, *Rocky Mountain News* real estate reporter John Rebchook interviewed him briefly about projects he was known to be considering in Denver.

Rebchook also questioned Trump's nattily dressed traveling companion, who had stood backstage during the tirade. He said his name was Felix H. Satter, and he made it a point to carefully spell it out with two *T*s.

Before Trump, his wife, and Satter got into a limo for the hour-long ride to Denver, Satter said Trump would be visiting the Denver Union Station redevelopment site. Satter obviously had an intimate familiarity with Trump's intentions—only the day before, Trump had said he had no plans to inspect the site. At the time, Rebchook thought nothing of the way the man spelled his last name. All he knew was that Satter was closely associated with Trump's plans in Denver.

"Satter's" name appears with just one *T* in a host of places. There's the deed to his home, for example. It is also spelled with only one *T* on New York State court papers from his 1991 felony conviction for stabbing a man in the face with the stem of a margarita glass.

The name Sater with one *T* also appears on federal court papers in a $40 million organized crime stock swindle he confessed to in 1998, a scheme that benefitted him as well as the Genovese and Gambino crime families. The stock swindle involved fake stock brokerage firms using high-pressure tactics to get naïve people to buy worthless shares from Sater and his mob friends.

The extra *T*, Sater later explained, was his attempt to conceal his past from people making simple Internet searches where his criminal history would be easily spotted. No doubt, Sater was also less than eager to have people in banking and real estate investments figure out that his father was a reputed Russian mob boss in Brooklyn.

Any effort to obscure his past ended in 2007, when real estate reporter Charles V. Bagli wrote a long *New York Times* article detailing Sater's criminal history and other dealings. Donald Trump, the Trump Organization, and Alan Garten (the general counsel) have all said that they check people out before doing business with them—a standard practice in business and a vital one for deals involving large amounts of money borrowed from banks and individual investors. Yet, until Bagli's article appeared, Trump and his lawyer said they had been unaware of Sater's criminal history.

Instead of severing ties with Sater, however, Trump continued to associate with him.

Sater worked for Bayrock, an investment firm involved in Trump SoHo, a luxury high-rise in Lower Manhattan, as well as a luxury high-rise on Florida's Atlantic Coast that was to be called Trump International Hotel and Tower Fort Lauderdale. The Florida project failed.

Curiously, Sater had no job title at Bayrock, whose offices were in Trump Tower.

When Sater left Bayrock, he moved into the Trump Organization suite of offices, also in Trump Tower. In 2010, three years after Bagli's article appeared, Sater was issued business cards by the Trump Organization. His title was "Senior Adviser to Donald Trump."

When people who had made advance purchases of condominiums in the high-rise found out about Sater's past, they filed a 2009 lawsuit against Trump and others. One of the issues was an alleged failure to be candid and forthright about who Sater was. The buyers asserted that failing to disclose Sater's criminal connections upfront was a violation of the duty to inform them of every material fact that could influence their decision to invest or walk away.

The suit (one of two over that project) also alleged that the whole high-rise endeavor was a classic bait-and-switch con job fostered with false advertising. The investors claimed that they had bought in only because Trump was the developer. It was supposed to be a quality Trump property, and they were willing to pay a premium price to invest in a building bearing the Trump brand. They later found out Trump had only licensed his name.

The civil racketeering suit also accused Sater of siphoning millions of dollars out of the project, harming the buyers while simultaneously hiding the proceeds from tax authorities. It was an accusation with more than a hint of the stock swindle that Sater had participated in, which the FBI said had benefitted him, the Genovese and Gambino crime families, and others.

Joe Altschul, a Fort Lauderdale lawyer representing seventy-five of the early Fort Lauderdale buyers, said his clients would never have deposited millions of dollars for their apartments had they known about Sater's criminal history. "Purchasers had a right to know who they were dealing with," Altschul said. "It's bad enough that they prop up Donald Trump as the developer, but then you find out it's not Trump but a convicted felon who had already been charged in financial shenanigans." According to Altschul, had Sater's past been disclosed, his clients "wouldn't have touched this deal."

Trump, under oath in the Fort Lauderdale lawsuit, expressed a different view, saying the failure of the project was actually a boon to the buyers. "On this one, they got very, very fortunate that they didn't put their money down, that they didn't buy the units and that would have been worth a fraction of what they were [worth] when they signed at the all-time high in the market," Trump explained.

Lawyers for the buyers noted that other Fort Lauderdale–area condo projects at that time were completed and had done just fine.

The 2009 lawsuit involving Trump International Hotel and Tower Fort Lauderdale happened to coincide with the sentencing for Sater's stock swindle. Sater had pled guilty in secret in 1998. Many of the court records of that case remain sealed in the federal courthouse in Brooklyn. For a file to remain largely sealed after almost two decades was so unusual that a retired federal judge, the *Miami Herald*, and others went to a higher court to get the records opened. It took a United States Supreme Court order to finally unseal some of the Brooklyn files in 2012.

Among the files that were finally made public was Sater's guilty plea to a felony charge in 1998. The files also included his 2009 sentencing—no jail time. Despite Sater's violent criminal past, he got probation plus a $25,000 fine. Aside from the relatively insignificant fine, there was no requirement that Sater pay back a cent of his ill-gotten gains.

There is every indication that the extraordinarily lenient treatment resulted from Sater playing a get-out-of-jail free card. Shortly before his secret guilty plea, Sater became a freelance operative of the Central Intelligence Agency. One of his fellow stock swindlers, Salvatore Lauria, wrote a book about it. *The Scorpion and the Frog* is described on its cover as "the true story of one man's fraudulent rise and fall on the Wall Street of the nineties." According to Lauria—and the court files that have been unsealed—Sater helped the CIA buy small missiles before they got to terrorists. He also provided other purported national security services for a reported fee of $300,000. Stories abound as to what else Sater may or may not have done in the arena of national security.

Without a doubt, Trump continued to be involved with Sater in business. In 2009, when the Trump SoHo opened in Lower Manhattan, video cameras captured Trump, microphone in hand, extolling the virtues of the project. Two men stood with him. One was Felix Sater.

Yet when the Associated Press asked about Sater in 2015, Trump said, "Felix Sater, boy, I have to even think about it." Earlier, under oath in videotaped testimony in the Florida case, Trump said he would not recognize Sater if he were in the room.

Other statements Trump has made under oath make it clear he knew about Sater's involvement with the CIA. The real problem for Trump—and what prompted him to distance himself from Sater—was liability for civil fraud in the Fort Lauderdale real estate litigation. The stronger the connection that the buyers in the failed project could establish between

Trump and Sater, the greater the damages they stood to collect from Trump.

Trump making money from deals, and then distancing himself from individuals he was involved with in those deals, was not limited to the lawsuit over the failed Fort Lauderdale project. As we shall see, it also came up in litigation over deals in Hawaii, Mexico, and Tampa.

22

—

DOWN MEXICO WAY

The sales pitches urged investors to get in early to reap the biggest profits. The Trump Organization, Donald himself, and two of his grown children announced that, along with a firm called Irongate and some other West Coast partners, they would soon transform a sleepy little spot on the Pacific coast—only a dozen miles from the California border—into the next hot Mexican vacation spot by building the Trump Ocean Resort.

The trump.com website listed Punta Bandera (which means "tip of the flag") as a "Trump Portfolio" property, one of thirty-three Trump Organization projects in "development" around the globe. A video and brochures touted the twin waterfront towers that would soon go up. Two of Trump's children flew to San Diego to mingle with would-be buyers.

"We are developing a world-class resort befitting of the Trump brand," Ivanka said in a video, between pictures of the Pacific Ocean, the beach, and renderings of the planned waterfront apartments. "We're really creating northern Baja as the new Cabo, as the new resort destination." She was referring to Cabo San Lucas, the once-quiet Mexican fishing village at the southern tip of the Baja peninsula, which, following the construction of waterfront hotels, now bustled with American tourists.

"This is a deal with my brother and, of course, our father, with the whole strength of the Trump Organization that we are extraordinarily bullish on," Ivanka continued. "Proximity to San Diego makes this a tremendous investment."

Trump himself appeared in the video as an authority on luxury development, saying, "I am very, very proud of the fact that when I build I have investors that follow me all over. They invest in me, they invest in what I build and that is why I am so excited about Trump Ocean Resort."

Prospective buyers were given a frequently asked questions sheet. One question: "Tell me more about the Developers, the Trump Organization and Irongate?"

Ivanka Trump told sales reception attendees that she was so impressed with the project that she was buying one of the apartments herself. She chitchatted with prospective buyers, saying that once they became neighbors she just might drop in to borrow some sugar. Her brother Donald Jr. also told prospective buyers he was buying his own pad.

The Donald Trump name and the assurances of his children attracted prospective buyers aplenty. Many paid a $5,000 deposit for an "Exclusive Priority Reservation Agreement," required just to hear a sales pitch at the Grand Hyatt in downtown San Diego. That payment was fully refundable to anyone who decided not to take advantage of the opportunity.

The prospect of getting in early on a transformative project, and one in which buyers might run into next-generation

Trumps, was so attractive to some people that they were neither put off by nor dubious of the high-pressure sales tactics. Much later, three people who had made exclusive priority reservations complained that they were given five minutes to buy or walk. That didn't even give them enough time to read the terms of their purchase contract, much less consult a lawyer. They signed, writing checks totaling more than $200,000. Some buyers later said they put their life's savings into their eagerly anticipated new homes by the sea. They came to regret being so hasty and so trusting.

Nearly two hundred people bought in, putting down more than $22 million in deposits in 2006, confident that the project was about to get underway and that before long they would move into their beachfront property and enjoy the security of a smart investment in a Trump-developed resort.

A June 2007 newsletter notified buyers that construction was underway. The next month, the *Trump Baja News* reported, "our new and excited homeowners now are part of an elite group of vacation homeowners who own property developed by one of the most respected names in real estate, Donald J. Trump."

Three months later, in October, when Wall Street crashed under the weight of toxic mortgages and other Baja real estate projects faltered, the same newsletter carried a message "From the desk of Ivanka Trump." Ivanka assured the buyers that their investment was sound. "Though it may be true that some of Baja's developments could slow down, these market conditions simply do not apply to Trump Ocean Resort—or any other Trump development," she wrote.

Two months later, in December 2007, the newsletter advised buyers of newly discovered geological problems afflicting the building site. A few months later, in March 2008, anxious buyers received calls or letters. Construction loans had been approved, would be funded shortly, and work would be underway. This was nine months after buyers had been told in writing that construction had already begun. Still, construction did not proceed.

All of these promotions, sales pitches, and newsletter updates created the impression that Trump was the builder and the developer, words he used. The buyers later said they bought in because Trump was the developer or builder. That understanding then changed abruptly.

The worst news arrived two days before Christmas 2008. What had previously been described as a partnership between "the Trump Organization, Donald J. Trump," and the other people and companies involved was described in a new way. Neither Trump nor the Trump Organization were investment partners in the Trump Ocean Resort. They were not the developers, either. They had merely licensed the use of the Trump name.

The actual Baja developers, it came out later, had "obtained authority" from Trump to use his trademarked name in return for an upfront fee. Under that licensing agreement, as testimony and court papers show, Trump gave the actual developer authority to tell prospective buyers that Donald Trump was "developing" the Mexico resort, even though he later testified that he was not. The losing buyers soon filed a host of lawsuits in California, asserting fraud and collectively demanding the return of their $22 million plus lawyers' fees and other costs.

The three people who faced the five-minute deadline to buy or walk away said in their 2010 court complaint that they went ahead only because Trump was the developer and had his own money in the deal—a belief strengthened by the statements that Ivanka and Donald Jr. were also buyers. Their lawsuit listed the Trump Organization first among the thirteen parties accused of California state securities fraud, simple fraud, negligent misrepresentation, accounting fraud, and unfair business practices.

In time, most of the lawsuits were consolidated in Los Angeles. The suits were revised and revised as new facts emerged until the fourth amended version of the complaint ran to more than 640 pages. It was filed on behalf of well more than one hundred buyers. The lawsuit detailed, by name, date, and event, each specific act of alleged deception used to get people to invest—a tactic that lawyer Daniel King said was meant to make sure there was no doubt about how pervasive the acts of deception had been.

In court papers, Trump distanced himself from the Baja deal. He insisted throughout that he never owed any obligation to the Baja buyers and had done nothing wrong. He also declared under oath in those cases, "I, personally, do not have any employees in the State of California, own real property in California, or maintain an office in California."

Trump in fact owned real estate in California, employed people in California, and had offices there. For years he had owned and operated his golf course on the Palos Verdes Peninsula in Los Angeles County. Testifying in a Florida federal case where other buyers had accused him of fraud in a similar waterfront condominium project, Trump was asked to name all the properties he owned. "Trump National Golf Club Los Angeles, I own that," he testified.

The crucial word in that California sworn statement was "personally." Trump did not own his California properties personally in the sense that most homeowners have their own names on the deed. Trump owned the golf course and employed people through a corporation, a corporation under his absolute control. Trump's lawyer at Trump National Golf Club Los Angeles was included on the list of people served with every document in the Baja litigation.

Daniel King, Bart Ring, and other lawyers for more than

one hundred of the buyers eventually made a deal with one of the non-Trump parties to pay back more than $7 million, a third of the buyer deposits. The Trump side objected that the deal was unfair to them and would leave them "holding the bag" for the other $15 million of deposits plus costs.

Trump's lawyers told the judge that his family and businesses never touched those deposits. The problem, they said, was that the *actual* developers did not have enough capital to complete the project. Trump's lawyers accused the real developers of misusing the deposits for personal gain by extinguishing personal debt guaranties related to the Trump Ocean Resort project. The license to use the Trump name, the Trump side pointed out, specifically prohibited Trump and his organization from doing any sort of developmental work. It barred them "from even inspecting the property on less than 'twenty-four hours notice' and required them to not 'interfere with the operation of the property.'"

"People who gravitate toward luxury brand name products do so because they expected superior quality and design," Trump's lawyer wrote. "They do not, however, believe that the designers are doing the 'dirty work.'" Furthermore, the lawyers wrote, while the buyers claimed that they were tricked into believing "that the Trump parties were the developer of the project," the buyers "could not have believed that Donald Trump would be on-site in Mexico overseeing construction or collecting their deposits . . .

"More importantly," the Trump lawyers continued, the license to use the Trump name "was disclosed to the plaintiffs when they entered into their contracts" and in the statement of how the condominium would be governed.

Trump's lawyers made no mention of testimony from buyers that they were given just minutes to sign the purchase and other documents, leaving no time to read them or ask questions about the several pages of arcane legal details. The only duty the Trump parties had, their lawyers wrote, was "to ensure that the standards of design and quality with the 'Trump' name were met, not to grade soil, dig ditches or collect deposits."

Trump, his organization, and his two children settled with the buyers. The court sealed the terms of the settlement.

Trump had been through all this before. A 2006 press release described Trump as "co-developer" of the Trump International Hotel and Tower at Waikiki Beach Walk, and a "partner" in the project. Reporters were told that the winner on Trump's television show, *The Apprentice*, would be "project manager overseeing development for Trump." Trump boasted that the combination of his name and Waikiki would be "setting a new standard of luxury." In late 2006, he bragged about "the biggest one-day sale in real history in the world" when buyers signed contracts totaling more than $700 million for 464 apartments.

Nearly three years after this successful one-day sale, when buyers were due to make the final deposits on their apartments, they received a brochure titled *Trump Waikiki Life, Owners Edition 2009*. On page twenty-three of the brochure, in what a lawsuit later described as "micro-script that can barely be read without a magnifying glass," people who had already signed sales contracts received troubling news: the Waikiki tower bearing the Trump name, in which many had invested their life savings, "is not owned, operated, developed or sold by Donald J. Trump, the Trump Organization," or any affiliated business. Trump had merely licensed his name.

Hawaii state law (like California and federal securities laws) protects buyers from false and misleading sales pitches. Hawaii law requires disclosure of all material facts to buyers. Trump's status as a mere licensor was obviously material to making an investment decision based on the supposed value the Trump name would add to the building.

But the licensing was not the most disconcerting fact that had been hidden. Long after they had made their deposits and signed contracts, the buyers discovered provisions in the Trump naming license that could jeopardize the future value of their apartments. Trump had reserved the right to take his name off the building. According to Trump's own statements, it was his name on the building that made the apartments so valuable; without it, the apartments would be worth much less. Furthermore, if Trump ever withdrew his name, he was free to put it on another building—even one right next door. This was crucial information to buyers looking to make a smart investment.

The lawsuit called this conduct unconscionable, citing more than twenty material facts that it said were improperly hidden from buyers. As with the Baja fraud suit, a settlement was reached and then sealed by a judge.

And in another Florida case (filed over a never-built Tampa high rise), buyers finally obtained a copy of the licensing agreement under court order. The licensing agreement stipulated that its very existence was to be kept secret—not just the specific terms of the agreement, but the existence of a licensing agreement in general. The agreement indicated that a Trump business was paid a $2 million upfront fee for use of the name.

In testimonies, Trump has named fourteen properties that are straight licensing deals and three others in which he also gets some profits or is a partial owner. In the Tampa case, Trump was asked about disclosures in other licensing deals:

"Do you, sir, or your company disclose to those buyers that you're merely licensing your name?" a lawyer asked.

"I think in some cases we do," Trump responded. "I am just not sure."

Another lawsuit was filed over a Fort Lauderdale hotel-and-apartment project that, at fifty-two stories, was to be the highest tower on the Florida Atlantic coast. Those buyers received a sales brochure with Trump's picture and the statement "It is with great pleasure that I present my latest development, Trump International Hotel and Tower Fort Lauderdale." Buyers also got hardcover books that announced on the first page: "A Signature Development by Donald J. Trump." The project failed and buyers wanted their deposits back. At trial in 2014, Trump testified that he had never claimed to be the developer and had no liability. "The word *developing* doesn't mean we're the developer," Trump said. The civil jury agreed. One of the buyers was still pursuing an appeal when this book was completed.

23

—

TRUMP BEACHES A WHALE

I t was almost four o'clock in the morning and Donald Trump couldn't sleep. For hours he had nervously paced the floor of his Trump Tower apartment, insisting on a call every thirty minutes with updates on the progress of a baccarat game in his first Atlantic City casino.

What kept Trump up all night was a Japanese gambler with a serene smile, a white shirt open at the collar, and gray wool slacks with pockets as big as bank vaults. Akio Kashiwagi was one of the world's five biggest gamblers, literally a one-in-a-billion customer, who at that late hour in May 1990 was sitting at a green-felt table at Trump Plaza Hotel & Casino calmly wagering $14 million an hour. He had been there for nearly a week.

Al Glasgow—a gravel-voiced concrete contractor who used to drink mob lawyers under the table in the days before he became one of Trump's closest advisers—called Kashiwagi "The Warrior." As the long hand on Glasgow's wristwatch approached the top of another hour, he stepped from behind the low black marble wall that separated the high-roller tables from the rest of the gambling floor and rang the boss in New York.

"He's up four point two," Glasgow said, not needing to add the word *million*.

Trump's anxiety would have been no surprise to those in the gaming world. Competitors (and even executives who worked for Trump) loved to swap stories about what he didn't know about the gambling business, from the odds of specific bets to the internal controls required to make sure no cash was skimmed off the top when the day's winnings were counted. And they loved to dish on Trump's awkward and uninviting behavior around gamblers.

The contrast between Trump and his rival, Steve Wynn of the Mirage resorts empire, was the sharpest. Wynn, a man of ego as monumental as Trump's, built a fortune as an expert card player possessed of a deep understanding of every casino game. His finely polished social skills matched his status as a world-renowned casino impresario.

Wynn would stroll through his casinos and restaurants with a small but informed entourage that fed him specific details about the next player they would encounter. He would approach a gambler, address him or her by name, and with a subtle flourish personally hand over the keys to a complimentary suite. Those few graceful moments gave the Indiana businessman or Georgia housewife who had come to a Wynn casino a valuable gift—bragging rights back home: *Steve Wynn personally gave me the key to my suite.* Wynn had perfected the art of efficiently making good customers feel special, building customer loyalty and attracting new players at far less cost than television advertising or paying junket organizers, though he used those too.

In contrast, Trump was often awkward with big customers. His germophobia kept him from shaking hands, and instead of flattering the customer, Trump typically turned conversations from the gambler to his own greatness.

What Trump liked about the gaming business was easy money, big easy money. Luring high rollers was one path to fat profits. But it was also a risky one. His former Trump Plaza casino partners, the company that grew from the Holiday Inn lodging chain and owned Harrah's casinos, preferred to target mid-level gamblers, especially slots players, who came, lost, and then came back again and again. This model generated steadier, lower-risk profits. When a Harrah's customer slipped her frequent player card into a slot machine, an automated message told a bartender to prepare the player's favorite drink. Soon a waitress would arrive with the refreshment, addressing the customer by name. One year, when the Holiday Corporation owned or franchised 1,589 Holiday Inns and other lodgings, it still earned twenty-eight cents out of every dollar of profit from its one Atlantic City casino.

Trump was more interested in flashy scores from big-name players than the secure profits that could be earned with intense management. He definitely wanted to lure The Warrior from his mansion near the foot of Mount Fuji—a house known locally as Kashiwagi Palace—to Atlantic City. When Trump flew to Japan in his aging Boeing 727 for the Mike Tyson–Buster Douglas world heavyweight championship fight in February 1990, he met The Warrior briefly. Trump presented his fellow real estate speculator with an autographed copy of his myth-making autobiography *The Art of the Deal*.

Casino executives in London, Las Vegas, and Darwin, Australia, all pursued Kashiwagi, one of that rare breed of gamblers known as "whales," because they risked $1 million or more during each casino visit. Kashiwagi—with his marathon multimillion-dollar sittings—remains, by far, the biggest whale ever beached in Atlantic City. Like the rest of the casino whales, Kashiwagi lived a financial life every bit as mysterious as the real denizens of the deep. The size and true source of his fortune were unfathomable.

Kashiwagi told Ernie Cheung, Trump's specialist in Asian marketing, that he was on a round-the-world gambling spree during which he was willing to risk $50 million. Other casinos desperately wanted to lure him to their floors. Caesars Atlantic City Hotel and Casino (which then vied with Trump Plaza as the top money winner on the Boardwalk) had invited Kashiwagi to drop in. Steve Wynn, the golden boy of Las Vegas gaming, wanted Kashiwagi to visit the Strip and try his luck at his brand-new Mirage, a giant ivory-trimmed gold box featuring a volcano out front, white tigers just off the casino floor, and, lest anyone forget its elemental purpose, a huge, shark-filled aquarium behind the registration desk. In this highly competitive market, Trump won Kashiwagi's action—though not in ways that would burnish his image as a deal artist.

The Warrior had visited Trump Plaza once before, twelve weeks earlier, when he won $5.4 million in one long day at the tables. Two months before that, Kashiwagi had flown to Darwin, where he had won the Australian equivalent of $19 million at the Diamond Beach Casino, bankrupting it. The Darwin results weighed on Trump, but he wanted to win back what he had already lost to The Warrior and more.

But, as Wynn and other casino executives knew, Trump did not understand the math of the games any more than he seemed to understand casino and hotel operations. For Kashiwagi's second visit to Trump Plaza, Trump paid $5,000 plus expenses to secure the advice of a mathematician who knew as much about casino games as anyone else on earth. Jess Marcum was an owlish little man who had helped invent radar in his youth, then became a founder of the RAND Corporation (the Air Force think tank), and later worked on the neutron bomb.

Though he didn't understand basic casino math, Trump did grasp one basic point: he was vulnerable to being cheated by players. Trump suspected that Kashiwagi had rigged the February baccarat game. Marcum and Glasgow studied videotapes made by cameras hidden in the smoky gray domes dotting the casino ceiling. Marcum quickly determined that Kashiwagi was no cheat. What fascinated Marcum were the subtle changes in Kashiwagi's face when he lost and how he never varied the size of his bets. "Turn off the [video tape] machine. I know how to beat him," Marcum said. "This guy loves a challenge. He's a natural for the freeze-out proposition."

The freeze-out, a double-or-nothing game, would have prevented Kashiwagi's earlier Trump Plaza payday. Double-or-nothing would appeal to The Warrior's love of a challenge, Marcum figured, and to his sense of honor. Most important, a double-or-nothing game would require him to keep gambling until he'd lost his entire pot. At the time, New Jersey mandated that casinos close for a few hours each day, and Marcum knew that Kashiwagi might contrive a reason not to return. A firm agreement, Marcum counseled, was required for the freeze-out proposition to work.

The deal had two parts. First, whatever money Kashiwagi brought to the table would be matched by a credit line, in effect doubling the gambler's pot. Second, once play started, Kashiwagi had to play one day after another until he either doubled his stake—his combined personal and borrowed money—or until he lost his last chip.

Marcum had been fascinated with gambling ever since a friend took him to see the horses run at Hollywood Park in 1953. Marcum quit RAND and started placing bets in Las Vegas. Within two years he had become wealthy. He was eventually banned from every betting parlor in town because he hardly ever seemed to lose. He had even managed a casino, but that was thirty years earlier, when he was young enough and foolish enough to think a great mathematical mind made for a great casino operator. With Trump, he was collecting a nice fee for advising a casino owner on how to run a game.

In May 1990, when Kashiwagi and his entourage arrived in Atlantic City for the second time, the casino expected him to bring $22 million in checks that could be verified easily and cleared through the banks. Instead, the only check that the casino would take—in a briefcase full of checks—was $6 million drawn on a Singapore bank. Kashiwagi asked for $12 million in credit. He got $6 million.

The maximum bet was set at $200,000 per hand, double what anyone else in Atlantic City had ever been allowed to wager. The Warrior was ready. Kashiwagi strolled across the bold red-and-gold Trump Plaza carpet to the high-roller area. An aide carried the fortune in chips in boxes under his arms. Uniformed security guards cleared a path, and onlookers gawked at how royally the big players were treated.

At Trump Plaza, Kashiwagi neatly arranged his huge cache of baked white clay discs flecked with red and blue. The chips cost $5,000 each and covered a large portion of the baccarat table. He put twenty in a stack, seven stacks to a row. Seventeen rows plus one extra stack of chips made $12 million in all.

That day, in all of the dozen Atlantic City casinos, all other players combined would lose only two-thirds the amount of money sitting on this one table. The $8 million the casinos would rake in would represent the losses of nearly one hundred thousand visitors to the seaside slum that calls itself the Queen of Resorts. One man had $12 million to gamble at Trump Plaza.

The neat stacks of chips drew hushed crowds to the low black marble wall that separated the high-roller tables from those for the hoi polloi. So impressive was Kashiwagi's play that hardly anyone noticed an elderly Hong Kong businessman with more than $1 million of chips at the baccarat table just to The Warrior's right.

Kashiwagi took a final puff on his Marlboro Light and set it down in the clean ashtray. The most voluptuous cocktail waitress in the casino appeared at his side. She bent low in her tiny black velvet suit, cut to resemble a merry widow, exchanged the ashtray for a clean one, and handed The Warrior a moist towel hot from a microwave placed on a table nearby just for him. The fifty-three-year-old real estate baron cleansed his face, returned the towel, and with a subtle nod signaled the dealer to begin.

Like Ian Fleming's James Bond, Kashiwagi favored baccarat. The object is to get nine points. Face cards and tens count as zero, aces count as one. There is no skill involved. Gamblers make only one decision: to bet for or against the bank. The game's fascination lies in the speed with which money changes hands, which explains why the French call their version *chemin de fer*, or "the railroad."

For six days Kashiwagi steamed down this track, betting $200,000 on each hand at the rate of seventy hands an hour, Trump fretting the whole time. Kashiwagi's bet never varied from opening until the casinos closed for four hours at six in the morning. The mandated closing was intended to give gamblers a chance to get a grip on their pocketbooks before the casinos picked them clean, a chance to get off that railroad.

Kashiwagi had no such concerns. He left the table only for meals, accompanied by his aides and a squad of casino security guards. A nearby restroom was closed to all other patrons, an "OUT OF ORDER" sign on the handle of a mop stuck in a bucket outside the door.

Most gamblers vary their bets. They believe in streaks. When they feel lucky, they double down; when they feel the cards are running against them, they cut back. Marcum thought this was all hokum at baccarat, in which probability, not skill, determines the outcome.

"There are no such things as lucky streaks," Marcum said, "but all gamblers believe in them." Almost all. Kashiwagi liked to make the same flat bet with every hand. He called his chips bullets, and he liked firing as many bullets as he could each time. Marcum knew this was the smartest way to bet. It was pure math.

Gambling has a rich mythology. From the earliest days of human society, casting lots—often by drawing straws or tossing dice made from the knuckle bones of sheep—was a way to ask the gods for answers. The high priest who wanted influence soon learned to become a "sharper," positioning the straws just right, shaving the dice, or even devising elaborate rules to ensure that more than random chance would determine the outcome. In many societies, it was a serious crime for anyone but the high priest to touch the instruments used to divine the will of the gods. This imbued the dice with a sacred quality. It also made sure no one could tell if they were loaded.

Most devoted gamblers still believed in that great and fickle goddess, Lady Luck. Many regarded casinos as a perverse kind of religious sanctuary in which their wins and losses revealed to them the Almighty's judgment. To such players, a casino was a temple of chance. In that respect, Marcum the mathematician was an atheist. In a confidential report to Trump, Marcum calculated that even with Kashiwagi's bold and smart betting style, the odds were five to one that the high roller would lose his bankroll before doubling it. The trick was to negotiate a deal that kept Kashiwagi at the baccarat table until he doubled his money or went broke.

On each bet the odds favored the house by a tiny margin. Again, the only decision in baccarat is to bet with the player or with the bank. The odds on a "player" bet favor the house by 1.36 percent; a "banker" bet favors the house by 1.17 percent. But the house also takes a 5 percent fee, called *vigorish*, on winning banker bets. Kashiwagi randomly switched between player and banker.

Marcum had endeared himself to the casino industry by inventing a new baccarat bet, the tie, which was lucrative beyond even the greedy imaginings of casino owners. Gamblers who bet that the bank and the player will get the same score—that is, a tie—have a chance to win seven dollars for each dollar they bet. But the odds of a tie are eight to one. That gives the casino a whopping 14.4 percent advantage on each tie bet. At Caesars Palace in Las Vegas, tie bets accounted for just 3 percent of baccarat wagers but 10 percent of what the house raked in. "It's a sucker's bet," Marcum told me. It was one bet Kashiwagi never made.

Even with the slim house advantages on the player and banker bets that Kashiwagi made, the player's bankroll should shrivel. The house advantage works like the reverse of compound interest, which makes a dollar saved grow over time.

After 10,000 hands, Marcum's calculations showed, Trump could expect to win 5,125 bets to Kashiwagi's 4,875. At that point, Kashiwagi would be out $50 million. The Warrior's actual $12 million stake would, in theory, disappear in many fewer hands.

"Probability is like a wave," Marcum explained, running his hand in a continuous up-and-down motion in front of his chest to indicate endless waves. "Because of the house advantage, over time the player dips lower and lower until he stops crossing the midpoint and ultimately loses all his money, unless he quits first."

Marcum's pages of handwritten numbers showed that after the first hour of baccarat, there was a 46 percent chance that Kashiwagi would be ahead. But after seventy hours of play, the likelihood that Kashiwagi would be winning would have shriveled to just 15 percent.

On the second day of Kashiwagi's marathon play in May 1990, however, his curve remained well above the line. Alarmed, Trump flew down from Manhattan the next day accompanied by global arms merchant Adnan Khashoggi, an Arab prince, and four vivacious blondes. Khashoggi was well-known in gambling circles, especially for all the unpaid markers he had left behind at the Sands in Las Vegas, which its chief executive blamed for that casino's collapse in 1983.

Trump, Khashoggi, and the others checked into Trump's Castle hotel, a few miles from the Boardwalk. That evening they limoed over to Trump Plaza. Trump introduced Khashoggi to Kashiwagi, saying they must have met because they traveled in the same circles. They had not. If he had paid more attention to the social aspects of running a casino—especially making big customers feel at ease—Trump would have known this.

Khashoggi sat down at the high-limit blackjack table next to Kashiwagi's baccarat table and began to play. Trump hung around, pumping hands and cocking his ears to every adulatory word from the gamblers beyond the marble wall. His behavior looked more like nervous pacing than his usual glad-handing.

Casino owners, favored by the odds, are not supposed to begrudge lucky players their winnings, they are not supposed to "sweat the action." And if they do sweat, they should do it from their executive offices, watching on a remote television screen, their anxiety hidden from the player. Within a quarter hour, Trump had grown restless and left.

Soon Kashiwagi was ahead $6.8 million. Together with the $12 million in chips he had bought, his pot now totaled $18.6 million—nearly halfway to doubling his money and winning the deal. His 3,720 chips took up more space than the green-felt table allowed, so rows of chips were arranged on the floor next to him. Crowds gathered along the low black marble wall just to stare at all the money. Kashiwagi, his back to them, seemed oblivious. He continued to wager steadily.

That night Trump panicked. He wanted the game stopped. He could stop it at any time by simply lowering the bet that the house would accept. Glasgow and everyone else involved knew that would be an insult and provoke Kashiwagi. He would almost certainly storm out, very comfortably in the black. Hoping to calm the casino owner—and keep him from appearing cowardly—Glasgow put Marcum on the phone to Trump.

"He's on a winning streak," Trump insisted, his voice gathering force for one of his frequent temperamental storms. "Is Kashiwagi cheating?"

"No," Marcum reassured him, Kashiwagi was no cheat.

"Be patient. He wants to keep playing, and soon the wave will run the other way." Trump said he would let the game go on a bit longer, but he wanted to know if Kashiwagi's pot continued to grow.

Kashiwagi was still ahead late the next week, but by only $4.4 million, down from his $6.8 million peak. The wave was moving in Trump's direction. In time, Marcum advised, Kashiwagi would lose all of the $12 million of chips he had begun with. Still, Trump could not sleep. He demanded the half-hour updates from Glasgow. Marcum, an old and now weary man, sat briefly at a table just outside the black marble wall, but a dealer made him get up, saying he had to play or stand, even though no other gamblers were waiting.

Kashiwagi knew the trend was going against him. He began saying he should get more credit, that he had been promised more credit so he could play with much more than the $12 million of chips he started with, even though half of those had been bought on credit.

The math, however, was not so neat, and Glasgow went home and fell into a brief, fitful sleep crunching the numbers. He had gotten the idea from me that the casino executives were wrong in their calculations of how much Kashiwagi was ahead or behind. Their numbers did not match the value of all the chips in the baccarat pit. Kashiwagi should have had about $480,000 more in chips at the table.

Glasgow called the Trump Plaza cage. "Anyone been cashing in five-thousand-dollar cheques?" he asked, using the casino term for such high-denomination chips that they bore serial numbers.

Well, yes, a clerk replied. Kashiwagi's translator and aide had cashed in $474,000 worth of them during the week. Glasgow was astounded. The cash-ins meant that Kashiwagi had converted nearly 10 percent of the credit chips into cash, money Trump Plaza would have a hard time getting back.

When Kashiwagi awoke that morning, he proposed that Trump extend him another $4 million credit. He needed more bullets to fire at his adversary. Ed Tracy, a polished executive who ran the Trump casinos at the time, met Kashiwagi in a lounge reserved for high rollers. Tracy, soon to be fired by Trump, would later run the incredibly profitable casinos that Sheldon Adelson owned in Macau. But Trump had a history of firing experts like Tracy and replacing them with less-experienced yes men.

The Warrior and Tracy sat near a large bronze Buddha that Trump Plaza had won from another high roller, Bob Libutti. Tracy explained that he was a simple man, not familiar with Japanese social graces, but that he was confident he and Kashiwagi could talk amicably as businessmen.

"You obviously have enough money to stay here and gamble forever," Tracy said. "But frankly, I don't want you to. I apologize if someone failed to fully negotiate the terms of the game, but our agreement stands." Kashiwagi was to play until he had won $24 million or lost it all.

Tracy knew from Marcum's pages of handmade calculations that the odds were eighty-seven to one against Kashiwagi coming back from his current state to double his original bankroll. He said no to the credit line increase. While the world still thought Donald Trump was a modern Midas, Tracy knew his boss had built a house of cards that could collapse if Kashiwagi won millions from the casino—just like the one in Australia.

Tracy said that while the credit line would not be increased after the current game ended, Mr. Trump would be honored to have his very best customer come up the Boardwalk to his brand-new Trump Taj Mahal casino. If that was of interest, they could initiate new discussions about how much cash and how much credit would make for a worthwhile game there. At the Taj, though, Tracy hinted, the maximum bet might be just $100,000, half of what Trump Plaza allowed.

Kashiwagi kept his counsel to himself. In an elevator reserved for him and his entourage, he descended to the baccarat table and resumed playing. Kashiwagi was down to six rows of $5,000 chips, a bankroll worth $4.2 million bought entirely on credit. Just after midnight, Kashiwagi lost a bet. Then another. And another and another until he had lost eleven in a row. Soon he won some money back. Just before the 6 a.m. closing time, when Kashiwagi was down to $2 million and change, The Warrior rose, bowed to the dealers, and left for the best suite in the house.

Glasgow sauntered to a telephone on the casino wall and called Trump with the news about Kashiwagi's bad luck.

"Isn't he great," Trump exulted. "He is really the greatest."

Kashiwagi was furious. Trump lacked honor, his aide, Daryl Yong, told casino reporter Dan Heneghan. Kashiwagi had come all the way from Japan after Trump presented him with a signed copy of *The Art of the Deal*, and now Trump was not honoring his promise of more credit. But the aide said Kashiwagi would get his revenge. "We plan to burn it soon," Yong said of Trump's autobiography.

Kashiwagi called Caesars next door, which provided him a limousine to depart Trump Plaza. Trump would later brag that he proposed that Kashiwagi return, that he come to the Trump Taj Mahal casino on the next Pearl Harbor Day, but that was hot air.

Kashiwagi had no intention of paying his marker. Word was spreading among casino executives that Kashiwagi was deeply in hock to the Japanese equivalent of the Mafia, known as the *yakuza*. He continued to seek high-profile deals at other casinos. Steve Wynn had him to the Mirage, though he was careful to limit Kashiwagi's credit and not put the house at risk.

Then on January 3, 1992, in the middle of the week long celebration of the New Year in Japan, an assailant entered the sprawling Kashiwagi Palace. Kashiwagi's family came home with fresh strawberries to find The Warrior on the kitchen floor in a pool of blood, his face hacked beyond recognition by a samurai sword, a ritual murder weapon employed by the *yakuza* when dealing with deadbeats.

Kashiwagi died owing Trump almost $6 million. This was on top of the $5.4 million he had previously won, plus the chips his aide had cashed in during the May visit, as well as the expenses of twice bringing the player and his entourage from Japan. Trump lost big.

Meanwhile, Trump was facing serious problems with an even bigger customer, one whose married daughter he kept trying to bed.

BIGGEST LOSER

Bob Libutti held a dubious honor among the thirty-three million people who played in Atlantic City during its mid-1980s golden age. He was the biggest loser of them all. He was also Donald Trump's best customer, and Trump treated him like a friend. Trump lavished gifts on Libutti, was generous with his time, and, less graciously, repeatedly tried to seduce the gambler's grown daughter.

A squat man in his fifties, Libutti had a dome head, a big nose, and the fast-talking style of the con man he was known to be. He told me that he started out with a sweetheart job as a waterfront truck driver before getting into racehorse deals. Libutti said people including George Steinbrenner, owner of the Yankees baseball team, paid him as much as a quarter-million dollars just to evaluate racehorses. In the early 1970s, he was banned from the racehorse industry after three dozen widely publicized horse trade scandals. According to the United States Tax Court, the horse deals—transacted between 1968 and 1971—involved civil tax fraud. Including penalties and interest, Libutti and his wife were ordered to pay just short of $1 million, equal to $6 million in 2016 money.

While he said his name was Robert Libutti, various investigations into his business practices by the racehorse industry and by Congress found that he had used other names, including Robert Presti and Nicholas Spadea. His birth certificate said Rafaele Robert Libutti.

In the early 1980s, Libutti mainly played at Caesars, where he stayed in the Emperor's Penthouse. There, in the hotel's finest suite, a table piled high with an incongruous mix of potato chips, lobster, and Dom Perignon would already be prepared for him on arrival. The champagne was chilled to the 43 degrees Libutti favored, and it was served in the Lalique crystal flutes that the casino had bought specifically for him. Casinos will provide these accommodations for someone willing to spend day after day wagering as much as $20,000 on each roll of the craps dice.

Donald Trump wanted those high-stakes rolls to happen at Trump Plaza, and to lure this whale he hired the salesman who had been handling Libutti's accommodations at Caesars. Libutti took the bait, walking the few hundred feet down the Boardwalk to Trump Plaza where he was treated like a dignitary. The salesman, security guards, and casino staff were waiting to see to his every need.

No one knew how deep Libutti's pockets were, but no one believed he had felt the seams. Trump was determined to reach into the deepest recesses of those pockets, and to do it he gave Libutti far more than just lobster and precisely chilled bubbly. To keep Libutti's lucrative business, Trump Plaza extended every privilege its best customer could imagine. Trump took Libutti on rides in his black Super Puma helicopter, brought him to the most exclusive sporting events and shows, and provided him a car and driver. When Edie Libutti—Bob's only daughter, a stylish divorcee to whom Trump was very attracted—turned thirty-five, Trump Plaza threw a lavish party including a professionally made video tribute. Donald Trump gave Edie a cream-colored Mercedes-Benz convertible for the occasion.

Steve Hyde, the Mormon elder who ran Trump Plaza casino, discouraged the lusty interest Trump took in Edie.

"Don't ever let him go out with her, Bob, don't ever," Hyde warned him.

"Why?" Libutti asked.

"You'll wind up killing him and you'll never come back here again," Hyde responded.

Furious that a married man would attempt to bed his daughter, Libutti confronted Trump, ordering him to stop asking her out. "Donald, I'll f---ing pull your balls from your legs," he threatened. Trump backed off, and Libutti continued pouring money into Trump Plaza.

One day Hyde called Libutti, urging him to come down to Atlantic City from his home in Saddle River, a wealthy North Jersey suburb where Richard Nixon lived a few blocks away. High rollers were supposedly beating the house big time, the gods of chance favoring the players instead of Trump, an argument that appealed to the superstitious player. Still, Libutti begged off, saying that his wife would kill him. He had lost too much money and Joan wanted him home. A limo soon showed up at Libutti's door with two women from Trump Plaza who told Joan they had come to take her on a shopping spree in Manhattan. Anything her heart desired, Donald would be glad to pay. "They'll do anything to get your money," Joan said. "They'll wreck your marriage if it will get them money."

Libutti played with cash, which meant the casino was not obligated to investigate the sources of his funding. Sometimes other players bought chips on credit and then passed them to Libutti at his table—players like a horse trainer who had a $200,000 credit line. Trump Plaza kept such detailed records of Libutti's play that it could determine his average 1987 bet to be precisely $13,929.52—but no one knew how many hundreds of thousands, or even millions, Libutti gambled and lost with chips obtained on other players' credit.

To keep gambling, Libutti required certain favors, known as comps or complimentaries, but Libutti's comps went far beyond the usual free suites and meals or, for select high rollers, helicopter rides to the casino and back. His demands were all satisfied, including a reliable $10,000 each month to pay his electric bill and the like: he received a monthly stack of show tickets from Trump Plaza, then traded them to a broker for $10,000 cash.

Trump Plaza also bought Libutti cars. Ferraris. Rolls-Royces. Whatever he wanted. The state's casino rules required that the casino buy the cars, but Libutti was free to instantly sell them back to the dealership, which would deduct a commission and then give him cash. Trump Plaza did not bother to arrange titles to the cars—the casino simply gave the car dealers checks. The dealers then took a fee and gave Libutti the rest. Libutti received $1.6 million this way. Because the sales were never registered, the dealers could still offer the cars as new. This was exactly the kind of ruse that the Casino Control Act was designed to prevent. It is illegal. And it went on for years.

When the dice hit Bob Libutti's numbers, he grew charming and generous. When it was time for his heart pills, the cocktail waitress who brought just the right water in just the right glass and presented her tray in just the right way could be rewarded with a black chip worth $100. Libutti told me he always kept a last $1,000 in his pocket to tip the helicopter pilots and other Trump staffers he needed to reward for their services. He said he started each morning by counting out fifty crisp hundred-dollar bills, holding them in a money clip made from a $5 gold piece minted in 1932, the year he was born.

When Libutti crapped out, though, his superstition joined with his temper to bring forth a vile magma of denunciations at the poor devils who caused his loss by looking at the dice the wrong way or speaking at the wrong moment. The dealers and waitresses and others assigned to Libutti's table ceased to be employees or servants or even human beings. They became "b----es" and "c--ts," "motherf---ers" and "c--ksuckers," "n----rs" and "k--es."

"Who the f--- do you think you are?" Libutti would rail, sometimes threatening to punch a dealer or use his influence to get the offender fired. No accusation was too absurd when Libutti's temper took hold—and no one doubted he could summon Trump instantly.

Whatever came out of Libutti's mouth, the suits expected the employees to stand there smiling, saying, "Yes sir, Mr. Libutti," so he would stay at the craps table until the cash he brought that day belonged to Trump. Nothing was to interfere with Libutti's compulsion to gamble. If Libutti insisted that some stupid #@!% dealer had called a cocked die wrong, that it was really leaning to a hard six and not a seven, management would interrogate the entire team working the table and let Libutti throw the dice again.

The highly regulated casino culture of Atlantic City forbade cocktail waitresses from accompanying players to their rooms, but if Libutti wanted five or six of them to come along and sip the best champagne, no one stopped him.

At Duke Mack's, Graybel's, and other watering holes where the dealers unwound over whiskey and beer, the way to outdo any tale of player foolishness was to recount the latest story about Libutti. The dealers called him Bob the Monster.

Bob Libutti said and did whatever he felt like, right down to demanding that Jim Gwathney, a Casino Control Commission inspector, get lost one Friday night. Gwathney's job was to make sure state regulations were being followed on the casino floor. He knew Libutti's reputation for abusing dealers and other workers. Libutti felt Gwathney was standing too close to him, but Gwathney stood his ground. Finally, Libutti threw several dozen black chips into the air, shouting "free chips." Afterward, Gwathney's bosses told him to stop hawking the game. They told him to stop being aggressive in inspecting. In effect, they told him not to do his job.

When Libutti was ahead and decided to quit and take his winnings (which wasn't often), he said there was always a problem with leaving. "The helicopter always had some mechanical problem and it would be fixed in a few hours or whatever other lie they could tell to keep me there. But if I ran out of money I'd turn to Rollo, my chauffeur, and I tell him to take the helicopter out to my house and get the attaché case with the seventy thousand dollars so I could keep playing." A helicopter was always ready.

"I'm a no-good degenerate gambler," Libutti told me in 1991 while enjoying his fourth twenty-five-dollar cigar of the day. His short frame sunk into his daughter Edie's feathery sofa, one of only six pieces of furniture in her living room the size of many houses, each wall more than thirty feet long. All around stood bronze statues of famous horses: Man o' War, Seattle Slew, Secretariat.

Seated with him were his wife Joan and her brother, the singer Jimmy Roselli, who grew up down the block from Frank Sinatra. Libutti opened another $200 bottle, the red wine as smooth as the cigars. The house belonged to his daughter, he claimed. So, too, he said, did Buck Chance Farm, a great name for a gambler's racehorse stable, even if it existed only on paper.

Trump and his casino staff, Libutti said, exploited his sickness, his compulsive gambling.

"They had me so entranced that they got me to the point where I started taking artifacts, antiques from the house, down there to gamble," said Libutti, Joan watching his every word, her eyes afire. "The jade Buddha that's in the chairman's suite at Trump Plaza cost me one hundred eighty-five thousand dollars. There's another Buddha, the bronze one that cost me forty-five thousand dollars." Trump Plaza arranged for a liquor vendor to buy the Buddhas and then sell them to the casino, Libutti said. "I got fifty some thousand for them. I went to the table, made two bets and lost it."

Libutti said he harbors no hatred of any group, that the language he used is the language of the streets where he grew up, and that he abhors racial discrimination. "The way I speak is vulgar, in the sense of common," he said. Besides, he added, if he was a racist, why did Mike Tyson give him the gloves he wore in one of his championship bouts held at Trump Plaza? Libutti said he never asked that a black or female dealer be removed, and the official state record supports that claim. Indeed, Libutti said when he was told that Trump had ordered that only white men work his tables in an effort to curry favor with his biggest customer he flew into one of his rages. Libutti said he used vile language, but the racist conduct came from Trump.

Libutti said he had realized a few years earlier that if he ever ran out of money to gamble, the state casino authorities would come after him, but that so long as he was losing they would look the other way at just about anything to keep Trump happy and collect 9.2 percent of his losses in casino taxes. After he ran out of money in late 1990, the state did just that, under the guise of banning Libutti because of his sexist and racist language. It was the first time anyone had been banned from a casino in New Jersey or Nevada for anything other than being a mobster.

The new chairman of the Casino Control Commission, Atlantic City politician Steve Perskie, asked the Division of Gaming Enforcement to file a petition banning Libutti. Commissioner Valerie Armstrong alone protested that Perskie's approach was improper. She said if there was to be any discipline it should be against Trump Plaza and other casinos for not ejecting an unruly customer. But Perskie prevailed in a 4-to-1 vote.

Mitch Schwefel, the enforcement division attorney assigned to make Libutti the one-hundred-and-fifty-second person banned from the Atlantic City casinos, knew he would have a tough time defending an exclusion in court if Libutti fought it on First Amendment grounds. But the state had other, more damning information.

Leonard "Leo" Cortellino and Charles Ricciardi Sr., both associates of the Gambino crime family, had told Robert Walker, a state police detective working undercover, about a bookmaking operation they ran in Atlantic City that benefitted the notorious Mafia don John Gotti. The bookies told Walker that they knew both Libutti and his brother-in-law. They said that Libutti "was in Donald Trump's pockets," explaining that Libutti had obtained a lucrative contract for Roselli at Trump Plaza for "big money." They also said Libutti was known to have run a number of scams with horses.

Libutti did indeed try to arrange a secret commission for Roselli's next singing gig at Trump Plaza during a September 1990 meeting with Ed Tracy, who in 1990 ran all three Trump casinos. Libutti felt that Trump owed him and he wanted a commission financed by inflating Roselli's contract. Libutti also asked about John Gotti coming to gamble at Trump Plaza. Since Gotti was not among the 150 mobsters the state had banned from Atlantic City's casinos, Libutti inquired about whether the dapper don would be welcome at Trump's.

Tracy had state police wire the room before he met Libutti again on July 31. I was Tracy's other appointment that day, but missed seeing Libutti by a few seconds.

"The problem that's remaining is the, ah . . . two hundred and fifty number," Tracy said.

"Right," Libutti answered.

"No way can I make that happen . . . My problem is a simple one. It's that the banks will see everything. Donald doesn't sneeze without them holding a handkerchief for him . . . We cannot make a deal that on paper doesn't make economic sense. They'd just throw it back at us and say, 'What's this?'" Tracy explained.

Their talk veered off to other subjects until Tracy smoothly steered it back to the payment Libutti wanted.

"So tell me how you want to structure this again?" Tracy asked.

"We'll take the money off Roselli's contract," Libutti said. "We'll say, listen, he wanted a thirty-thousand-dollar increase per show . . . so you got him to do the show for the same fifty-six thousand five hundred dollars, with a bonus if he signed for a year . . . and I get the bonus of a quarter million dollars."

Libutti later insisted that he was "only puffing" and had never met Gotti, though he added, "he's the kind of guy I should like to be around. I admire the guy."

Trump told me in 1991 that he was only vaguely familiar with Libutti and could not identify him if he were in a group of two. That is a common Trump defense, one he has used again and again. Trump boasts he has "the world's greatest memory," but when a connection turns out to be a problem, Trump will assert that he cannot remember someone or that he knew them so tangentially that he could not identify them in a crowd of two. In this case there were photographs, casino records, and that birthday video for Edie showing Trump knew Libutti quite well.

"He's a liar," Libutti said, spewing four- and seven- and thirteen-letter insults about Trump when he learned of this distancing.

Libutti added that he was aware of all sorts of serious rules violations at Trump Plaza that would be of interest to the casino regulators. He told one story of Donald Trump coming to him on the casino floor and personally handing him a $250,000 check. "As I'm checking out . . . they call Donald. He goes in his pocket and takes out the f---ing check and goes, 'I want to present this to you myself.'"

Such an incident would have been captured on the surveillance cameras in the smoky grey domes that dot casino ceilings.

"Now you tell that one to Sweeney," Libutti said, referring to Jack Sweeney, whom Chairman Perskie had handpicked to be the Division of Gaming Enforcement director. "And when Sweeney hears it you know what he'll say. He'll say, 'Bob

Libutti doesn't have any credibility and we're not going to look into it.' Well, he doesn't need Bob Libutti because when Donald gave me that check there was a whole casino full of witnesses."

In February 1991, I advised Sweeney of Libutti's claim that Trump had personally handed him a check.

"Well, if that was true it would be very serious," Sweeney told me, "but Libutti's got no credibility."

Sweeney was then told that Libutti had anticipated that response and was told about the other witnesses.

"Well, that'll be thoroughly investigated," Sweeney added.

The investigation into the check marked the first time that Donald Trump had ever personally been the subject of an enforcement division investigation. It did not last long. Several of the witnesses Libutti identified said they were never contacted, never questioned. Sweeney's office did call in one witness and asked him about the accusations under oath. The witness was Donald Trump. He denied the accusations. Trump said the check in question had been turned over, but in a perfectly legitimate way. Sweeney took his word for it. That cleared Trump completely. No action was taken.

The commission soon voted to ban Libutti, not for his vile remarks, but for saying he knew John Gotti.

The Casino Control Commission ultimately fined Trump Plaza for discriminating against its own workers and for deceiving the commission with fake-gift cars that were used to funnel cash to Libutti. The Commission also made clear what it thought about the offense of money laundering versus discriminating against women and minority employees. Trump Plaza was fined $200,000 for racial and gender discrimination and $450,000 for sham car deals.

The state deftly avoided investigating the more extensive wrongdoings that Libutti said he knew about. If proven, those claims would surely have cost Trump his license. Trump's conduct with Libutti, including his claim that he hardly knew the man, was just one part of a long history of flouting the supposedly strict regulations of New Jersey casinos. But even the strictest rules only matter if they are enforced.

As the many episodes recounted in these pages have shown, Trump is remarkably agile at doing as he chooses and getting away with it.

EPILOGUE

N o book can capture the entire life of someone who has done half as much as Donald John Trump has in his seventy years. Through sheer force of will, he has made himself a household name and left a dramatic mark on both the biggest city in America and a much smaller one along the New Jersey shore. He has reveled in every bit of it.

As I noted in the introduction, I would be writing a book about Hillary Clinton but for the simple fact that in 1988, my career took me not to Little Rock, Arkansas, but to Atlantic City, New Jersey. Others have written books on Mrs. Clinton, and I encourage people to read them.

What I have attempted to do here was take my direct knowledge of Trump and the many thousands of pages of Trump documents I've collected in my nearly half a century as an investigative reporter, and focus on the aspects of Trump's conduct that I think are most important for voters to ponder before they cast their ballots in November 2016. In winnowing down all the things I wanted to convey about Trump, I kept in mind two critical lessons for writers generally, plus a third for investigative reporters specifically:

Brevity, first and always, through the use of revelatory details and events, not every detail and every event.

Second, a lesson from F. Scott Fitzgerald, one of the most perceptive of American observers: action is character. Throughout this book, I have made reference to Trump's conduct. We can never truly know his character, but we can examine and assess it based on his actions.

This is why I focused on Donald Trump's obsession with money and the trappings of wealth, as well as his many comments about women not as equals, but objects, their value measured in particular by the size of their busts and the length of their legs.

That is also why so much of this book is about Trump's many complex and little-known relationships with criminals—a vast assortment of con artists, swindlers, mobsters and mob associates, a major drug trafficker he went to bat for, and other unsavory characters. Merely knowing people who are criminals is not the basis for condemnation. I've spent many hours of my life with crooked cops, drug dealers, pimps, prostitutes, police spies, foreign agents, and other rogues. They have been among my best sources. When it suits their interests, crooks can be among the most trustworthy allies. The man the FBI said was the No. 2 hitman west of Chicago once sat in my kitchen, bouncing my then-infant fourth daughter on his knee while I made coffee. He was no threat to me; I was outside the subculture that employed him as enforcer of its rules.

As these pages make clear, Trump's relationships with criminals were often profitable, sometimes gratuitous, and never properly examined by those whose duty was to investigate.

Third, the skeptical credo of investigative reporters: If your mother says she loves you, check it out. Then cross-check and cross-check again and again until you have the facts bolted in their proper place within the universe of the verifiable. Investigative reporting is about facts that are not announced in press releases or spoken in presidential addresses, but that lurk in the dark crevices of government, business, and human relations. It is a trade in which the calling is to shine bright and focused light into unwelcome places for society's benefit.

It is not surprising, at least to me, that Trump is always attacking journalists as unfair and banning news organizations from his rallies over something they reported or how they reported it. I was not surprised when he threatened (again) to sue me. His threats help take the edge off most journalism about him. Donald Trump is not a man who tries to understand how others perceive him. Rather, he dismisses those who do not see him as he sees himself. In this he is a world-class narcissist.

While I was working on this book, Steve Weinberg, the former executive director of the training organization Investigative Reporters & Editors, wrote that he considers me among the six best investigative reporters of his lifetime, a judgment I am sure others would dispute. He also wrote that he sees a parallel between Trump and me in that we have both led colorful lives. No one who knows me and knows about Trump would question that.

Trump and I are alike in another way as well, which is one reason I was intrigued from the moment I met him in June 1988: we each do things our own way and don't have anyone as our boss, as many an editor who has worked with me can attest.

Where we differ is in what we value. Donald Trump is all about money, a love that his conduct amply demonstrates without his constant reminders that he's really, really, really rich. Or so he says. I value honor. Faced with a choice between the two, just as Trump is compelled to choose money, I am compelled to choose honor. Once lost, honor might never be regained; more money can always be earned.

Trump's love of money is one of many traits that I hope readers better understand after reading these pages. I hope they will evaluate the prospect of a Trump presidency.

In doing as he chooses without regard to the rules that restrict the behavior of others, Trump has made himself a hero to some, a pariah to others. Whether one adores Trump or is aghast, his public conduct should prompt us all to think about what qualities we want in our political leaders and why there is so much opportunity for someone like Trump to garner tens of millions of votes. We should ask ourselves why so many Americans are excited at the prospect of someone whose public statements show utter disregard for the checks and balances that buttress our system of self-government—a system that has made America, flaws and all, a beacon to the world for more than two centuries.

Many of the things Trump says he would do if elected are not within the limited powers we grant presidents. Presidents cannot unilaterally spend taxpayer money, cannot impose tariffs on foreign goods, and cannot dictate to corporations where they will invest. They also cannot expect soldiers to follow illegal orders, as Trump has said he would demand, from the use of torture—prohibited by our Constitution and the treaties that are the law of the land—to the killing of innocent civilians, notably the children of terrorists he describes as Islamic (terrorists whom I consider Muslim apostates who describe themselves in their own publications as apocalyptic believers expecting the world to end soon).

Businessmen can, as Trump often does, dismiss people and move on. Presidents do not enjoy that luxury. They must contend with ever-present forces that are not subject to their control. A president cannot dismiss a troublemaking foreign head of state, cannot order Congress to pass laws, and cannot disobey the rulings of judges—not if we are to be a free people, living subject to the rule of law that protects our individual liberties. Yet Trump makes clear that he would do all these things. His vision is, in many ways, not that of a president but of a dictator, as many others have observed in both political parties and beyond America's borders.

I also hope the reader has grasped the reasons I focused on Trump's own extensive words and public statements about revenge. His clear and repeatedly articulated personal motto is to take that which Jesus said belongs only to God— vengeance. One need not be a believer to notice how at odds Trump's many statements on religion are with the teachings of the Bible, Old Testament and New, and thus with his claim to be a Christian.

Trump says he does not see any reason to seek divine forgiveness because he has done nothing wrong in his entire life, an oft-made observation so at odds with the most basic teachings of Jesus that I am at a loss to explain any religious leader embracing him. Trump's own words are aggressively antithetical to the teachings of the New Testament. His understanding of the one Old Testament phrase he knows is warped at best. Now factor in his statements denigrating communion—"I drink my little wine, eat my little cracker"— and his fumbling pronunciation of Paul's second letter to the believers in Corinth, and weigh them against his claim that he reads the Bible more than anyone else. These are signs of a deceiver.

Trump's success with voters tells an important story about the deep trouble America is in. His rise illustrates the growing chasm between America's political leaders and the rest of the country. So does the success of Bernie Sanders, who often drew bigger crowds than Trump during the 2016 primaries.

Both men tapped into a frustration I have chronicled for decades, writing extensively about inequality for many years before it became a household concern. While both Trump and Sanders can rally people, neither has put forth actual policy proposals that could move America from where things are to a fairer, more just, and widely prosperous society. Nothing in their pasts suggests that they have the political skill to wring change from the system if elected to the presidency. Hillary Clinton has the skill, but despite her decades of action on behalf of the less fortunate, it is not at all clear that this is foremost on her political agenda.

Whatever your views, become deeply informed. The Founders believed that knowledge and reason must be the cornerstones of our representative democracy if we are to govern ourselves. So spend time learning and then do your duty as a citizen. Vote.

David Cay Johnston
July 4, 2016
Rochester, New York

ACKNOWLEDGMENTS

N o one practices investigative journalism alone. For nearly half a century, my work has benefitted from the generosity of an astonishing array of people. Cops, file clerks, waitresses, drug dealers, pimps, prostitutes, and spies, as well as professionals and professors and executives in business, government, and nonprofits. Quite a few were successful business owners. Many of these sources took risks to get information to me, trusting that I would make the best use of it for the public good.

This book draws on help from many people during my nearly three decades of observing Donald Trump and collecting Trump documents. My insights about him come in part from a life of deep study in economics and management as well as tax and regulatory law, the principles and theory of which I have been privileged to teach since 2009 at Syracuse University College of Law and Whitman School of Management. I am not a lawyer, accountant, or MBA. Indeed, I don't have a college degree, just seven years of full-time study, heavily weighted to upper division and graduate-level courses, including at the doctoral level.

First among the many people whose contributions I must acknowledge is my third daughter, Amy Boyle Johnston, an artist and author of *Unknown Serling*, the first volume in her myth-busting study of Rod Serling's enduring contributions to American culture. Her research skills and grasp of both legal theory and nuances of language were a tremendous help. I appreciate all the time she donated. Her twin brother, Andy, provided reminders about our dealings with Trump.

My eighth grown child, the comedy writer Kate Leonard, offered valuable research and criticism, applying the language skills that got her hired straight out of college as script coordinator for the Netflix series *House of Cards*. My fourth daughter, Molly Leonard, a Canadian lawyer, applied her keen eye to parts of the manuscript. My oldest son, Marke, a lodging company entrepreneur whose insights have been the inspiration for scores of news articles in major newspapers reported by me and others, played a crucial technical role by digitizing thousands of pages of paper files belonging to Wayne Barrett and to me.

Barrett, arguably the best reporter ever in New York City and whom I revere as if he were a big brother, generously made his digitized files available to many journalists doing the important work of vetting the candidate. I also benefitted from Wayne's deeply informed, unsparing, and wise counsel.

Libby Handross, whose documentary *Trump: What's the Deal?* that Donald Trump suppressed with litigation threats in 1991, graciously provided me with early access to the film and advice in tying down key facts. But for a lengthy film proposal that director Tim Burton retained me to write many years ago, I would not have thought through many of the connections that I hope readers of this book find helpful in understanding Trump.

In California, novelist and short story writer Cindy Santos diligently dug through court files, as she did for one of my earlier books. Journalists Dana Kennedy and Danelle Morton gave sage advice on tone and what to leave out.

Dennis Johnson, co-founder with Valerie Merians of Melville House Publishing, and my longtime literary agent Alice Fried Martell were the artists of this book deal. Editors Ryan Harrington and Taylor Sperry helped focus and polish my words in the very fast-paced production of this manuscript. Zachary Gresham performed the vital and often unappreciated work of copyediting, while Holly Knowles created the index, and David Chesanow proofread it all. Alan Kaufman legally vetted my work. Fritz Metsch designed the book's interior, and Archie Ferguson designed the jacket art, with a simple elegance I love, with art director Marina Drukman overseeing their efforts. Simon Reichley helped keep the production schedule on track. Supervising them all was managing editor Wah-Ming Chang.

This book and my first book, the 1992 casino industry exposé *Temples of Chance*, would not have been possible without the generosity of the late Al Glasgow, a Trump consultant mentioned in these pages; lawyer David Arrajj; *Philadelphia Inquirer* journalists Bill Marimow, George Anastasia, Mike Schurman, and Bill Sokolic, as well as Dan Heneghan, then a journalist from the *Press of Atlantic City*; and physicians Marvin Hoffman and Clive Zent. Many other people who asked me back then not to name them provided documents and invaluable explanations and insights.

I am grateful to the editors who improved the two dozen

columns and articles I wrote for various national publications beginning just days after Donald Trump announced his candidacy: Joe Conason of *National Memo*, Michael Hirsh of *Politico*, Jim Impoco of *Newsweek*, David Johnson of the now-defunct *Al Jazeera America*, Jill Lawrence of *USA Today*, Harry Shearer and John Avalon of *The Daily Beast*, as well as Caleb Silver and Julia Kagan of *Investopedia*.

My best friend, the enterprising former *Wall Street Journal* and *Los Angeles Times* editor David Crook, and his wife, the witty writer Lauren Lipton, gave encouragement and advice.

As always, my wife, Jennifer Leonard, despite her duties as CEO of the Rochester Area Community Foundation and her tireless advocacy for those born into tough circumstances, gave her unvarnished criticism, as she has throughout a wonderful marriage that after thirty-four years has not lasted nearly long enough.

NOTES

Any reader who encounters a broken link in trying to review any source document listed in these notes may e-mail me at davidcayjohnston@me.com. I will do my best to promptly get you a working link or a copy of the document.

CHAPTER I. FAMILY HISTORY

4 **In 1892, Friedrich became a citizen, lying about his age:** Julie Muhlstein. "Trump's Grandfather Won an Election Too—In Monte Cristo." Heraldnet.com. www .heraldnet.com/article/20160303o9/BLOG60/160309162.

4 **Friedrich was the genesis of many Trump family traditions in America:** Blair LoBianco, "Trump Children Unable to Vote for Dad in NY Primary." CNN, April 12,

2016. www.cnn.com/2016/04/11/politics/donald-trump-ivanka-vice-president/.

5   **A family tradition Friedrich Trump did start in America, however:** Tracie Rozhon, "Fred C. Trump, Postwar Master Builder of Housing for Middle Class. Dies at 93." *New York Times*, June 26, 1999. See also Gwenda Blair, "The Man Who Made Trump Who He Is." *Politico*, August 24, 2015. www.politico.com/magazine/story/2015/08/the-man-who-made-trump-who-he-is-121647.

6   **Hoping the fortune he brought into the country would impress the authorities:** Gwenda Blair, *The Trumps: Three Generations of Builders and a Presidential Candidate.* Digital: LOC 1677.

7   **Back in New York City, Frederick continued to prosper:** Blair, LOC: 1924.

CHAPTER 2. FAMILY VALUES

9   **Though only twelve years old when his father died in 1918:** Tracie Rozhon, "Fred C. Trump, Postwar Master Builder of Housing for Middle Class. Dies at 93." *New York Times*, June 26, 1999.

9   **getting himself arrested at age twenty-one for his involvement in a battle:** Matt Blum, "1927 News Report: Donald Trump's Dad Arrested in KKK Brawl with Cops." *Boingboing*, September 9, 2015. boingboing.net/2015/09/09/1927-news-report-donald-trump.html.

10 **Almost nine decades later, his son Donald, running for President:** Jason Horowitz, "In Interview, Donald

Trump Denies Report of Father's Arrest in 1927." *New York Times*, September 22, 2015.

11 **During World War II, Fred Trump landed Government contracts for apartments and barracks to be built:** Rozhon, "Fred C. Trump, Postwar Master Builder of Housing for Middle Class. Dies at 93."

12 **He was also something of a showman, displaying the panache:** Rozhon, "Fred C. Trump, Postwar Master Builder of Housing for Middle Class. Dies at 93."

12 **Decades later, of course, Donald Trump would surround himself with models:** "10 Secrets of Fred Trump's Coney Island Revealed in History Project Exhibit." Coney Island History Project, May 26, 2016. www.coneyislandhistory.org/blog/history/10-secrets-fred-trumps-coney-island-revealed-history-project-exhibit.

12 **Years later came a stunt that would appear to be a direct inspiration to his son:** Michael D'Antonio, "Ike Didn't Like Donald Trump's Dad." *Daily Beast*, November 23, 2015. www.thedailybeast.com/articles/2015/11/23/ike-didn-t-like-trump-s-dad-at-all.html.

13 **Testifying before the Senate Committee on Banking and Currency, Fred Trump insisted:** Hearings before the Committee on Banking and Currency, United States Senate, Eighty-Third Congress, second session, pursuant to S. Res. 229.

14 **Taxpayers were not the only source of capital for Fred Trump's construction projects:** Leonard Buder, "Two with Links to Crime Group Charged by U.S." *New York Times*, September 11, 1986.

15   Fred Christ Trump was a stern father who expected his sons to learn the family business: Rozhon, "Fred C. Trump, Postwar Master Builder of Housing for Middle Class. Dies at 93."

16   As first-born, Fred Jr. was first in line to rise in dad's business: Jason Horowitz, "For Donald Trump, Lessons from a Brother's Suffering." *New York Times*, January 2, 2016.

17   Meanwhile, Fred Jr. had become a pilot for TWA: Horowitz, "For Donald Trump, Lessons from a Brother's Suffering."

18   With the way now open to becoming next in line in the family business: Michael Rothman, "Actress Candice Bergen Opens Up About Past 'Blind Date' With Donald Trump." Abcnews.go.com, February 12, 2016. abcnews.go.com/Entertainment/actress-candice-bergen-opens-past-blind-date-donald/story?id=36892025.

18   Others have said they don't recall seeing Trump a lot around campus: Mark Dent, "Donald Trump, Penn Grad, Is (Barely) Remembered by His Alma Mater: 'Who Wants to Be Associated with Him?'" Billypenn.com, July 30, 2015. billypenn.com/2015/07/30/donald-trump-penn-grad-is-barely-remembered-by-his-alma-mater-who-wants-to-be-associated-with-him/.

CHAPTER 3. PERSONAL VALUES

21   A violent convicted felon and swindler named Felix Sater: Charles V. Bagli, "Real Estate Executive with Hand in Trump Projects Rose from Tangled Past." *New*

York Times, December 17, 2007. Accessed June 20, 2016. www.nytimes.com/2007/12/17/nyregion/17trump.html.

21 **helping Trump make two major development deals in Denver:** John Rebchook, "Trump Looks for Land to Build Hotel, Condos." *Rocky Mountain News*, July 8, 2006. Accessed June 20, 2016. www.denverinfill.com/images/blog/2006-07/2006-07-08_trump_looks_for_land_to_build_hotel_condos.pdf.

21 **Trump and Sater gave interviews to the *Rocky Mountain News*:** John Rebchook, "Trump Thinking Big for Denver." *Rocky Mountain News*, September 15, 2005. Accessed June 20, 2016. www.highbeam.com/doc/1G1-136190082.html.

22 **He ripped into the location and functionality of the Denver International Airport:** Andy Vuong, "The World According to Trump." *Denver Post*, September 15, 2005.

22 **described her as "ugly as a dog":** Christine Steele, "Trump Talks Frankly for Front Range." *Daily Reporter-Herald* (Loveland, CO), September 15, 2005.

22 **"I love losers because they make me feel good about myself":** Tony Kindelspire, "'The Donald' Makes an Appearance at Loveland Bixpo." *Daily Times-Call* (Longmont, CO), September 15, 2005.

22 **three dollars rather than the "feaking fortune" paid to Trump:** Vuong, "The World According to Trump."

22 **"because they are gonna try to fleece you":** Tom Hacker, "Trump's Bixpo Show Offends—but It's Show Biz." *Biz West*, September 30, 2005. Accessed June 20,

2016. bizwest.com/trumps-bixpo-show-offends-but-its-show-biz/.

22   **Trump has been a party in more than 3,500 lawsuits:** Nick Panzenstadler and Susan Page, "Exclusive: Trump's 3,500 Lawsuits Unprecedented for a Presidential Nominee." *USA Today*, June 2, 2016. Accessed June 5, 2016. www.usatoday.com/story/news/politics/elections/2016/06/01/donald-trump-lawsuits-legal-battles/84995-854/.

23   **"Boy, do I feel good" . . . "I always get even" . . . "She bought a beautiful home" . . . "'Donald, I can't do that'" . . . "I was really happy when I found that out":** Hacker, "Trump's Bixpo Show Offends—but It's Show Biz."

24   **Rosie O'Donnell, who described him as "a snake-oil salesman":** Cady Drell, "A Brief History of Donald Trump and Rosie O'Donnell." *Newsweek*, August 6, 2015. Accessed June 8, 2016. www.newsweek.com/behind-donald-trumps-sexist-debate-comment-rosie-odonnell-pigs-fat-view-360701.

24   **and later (on television) "disgusting inside and out":** Donald Trump and Bill Zanker, *Think Big: Make It Happen in Business and Life* (New York: HarperCollins, 2009), p. 188.

24   **He made disparaging remarks about her looks, weight, and sexuality:** Trump and Zanker, *Think Big*, p. 189.

24   **"You've got to hit a bully really hard really strongly, right between the eyes":** Trump and Zanker, *Think Big*, p. 190.

24   "Attack them in spades": Trump and Zanker, *Think Big*, p. 194.

24   "No one reads the Bible more than I do": Jesse Byrnes, "Trump: Kerry Probably Hasn't Read the Bible." *The Hill*, February 24, 2016. Accessed June 6, 2016. thehill .com/blogs/blog-briefing-room/news/270610-trump-kerry-probably-hasnt-read-the-bible.

24   He says *The Art of the Deal* is the greatest book ever written except for the Bible: Blake Hounshell, "Trump Bungles Bible Reference at Liberty University." *Politico*, January 18, 2016. Accessed June 20, 2016. www.politico.com/story/2016/01/trump-liberty-university-bible-217938.

24   He has never been able to recite a biblical verse: Eugene Scott, "Trump Says Bible Is His Favorite Book but Declines to Share Favorite Verse." CNN, August 27, 2015. Accessed June 6, 2016. www.cnn.com/2015/08/27 /politics/donald-trump-favorite-bible-verses/.

25   Trump told Bob Lonsberry, a radio host in Rochester, New York, that he was religious: "Bob Lonsberry Talks with Donald Trump." WHAM1180.iheart.com, April 14, 2016. Accessed June 26, 2016. wham1180.iheart.com /onair/bob-lonsberry-3440/bob-lonsberry-talks-with-donald-trump-14604930/.

25   "Well, I think many . . . we can learn a lot from the Bible, that I can tell you": "Bob Lonsberry Talks with Donald Trump." WHAM1180.iheart.com, April 14, 2016. Accessed June 26, 2016. wham1180.iheart.com/onair /bob-lonsberry-3440/bob-lonsberry-talks-with-donald-trump-14604930/.

26 "My motto is: Always get even": Trump and Zanker, *Think Big*, p. 183.

26 "If you don't get even, you are just a schmuck! I really mean it, too": Trump and Zanker, *Think Big*, p. 190.

CHAPTER 4. A SICKLY CHILD

27 Two of Donald Trump's mottos, "Always get even" and "Hit harder": Jason Horowitz, "For Donald Trump, Lessons From a Brother's Suffering." *New York Times*, January 2, 2016.

28 A letter from a Trump family lawyer instructed Precise: Heidi Evans, "Inside Trump's Bitter Battle; Nephew's Ailing Baby Caught in the Middle." *New York Daily News*, December 19, 2000.

28 Fred Trump Senior had been diagnosed with Alzheimer's in 1993: Tracie Rozhon, "Fred C. Trump, Postwar Master Builder of Housing for Middle Class. Dies at 93." *New York Times*, June 26, 1999.

29 Fred Sr.'s lawyer had drawn attention to the potential for litigation over the estate: Evans, "Inside Trump's Bitter Battle; Nephew's Ailing Baby Caught in the Middle."

29 The lawyer asked Fred Sr. to fill out a routine estate planning form that described his intentions: Evans, "Inside Trump's Bitter Battle; Nephew's Ailing Baby Caught in the Middle."

29 she "burst out into tears" on learning her sickly son was in jeopardy: Evans, "Inside Trump's Bitter Battle; Nephew's Ailing Baby Caught in the Middle."

29 A judge signed an order directing the medical cover-
    age continue until the matter could be resolved: Linda
    C. Trump, et al. v. Donald J. Trump, et al. No. 6795/00.
    Supreme Court, State of New York.

30 Donald said he was doing nothing but carrying out
    the wishes of his father: Evans, "Inside Trump's Bitter
    Battle; Nephew's Ailing Baby Caught in the Middle."

31 Maryanne Trump Barry weighed in, too: Linda C.
    Trump, et al. v. Donald J. Trump, et al. No. 6795/00. Su-
    preme Court, State of New York.

31 Years later, while seeking the Republican presidential
    nomination: Ray Nothstine, "Donald Trump: 'I'm Not
    Sure If I Ever Asked God's Forgiveness.'" Christian Post,
    July 20, 2015. www.christianpost.com/news/donald-
    trump-im-not-sure-if-i-ever-asked-gods-forgiveness-
    141706/.

31 Trump said his pique at the challenge to his father's
    will motivated the termination: Jason Horowitz, "For
    Donald Trump, Lessons From a Brother's Suffering."
    New York Times, January 2, 2016.

CHAPTER 5. MAKING FRIENDS

33 Trump has boasted often that he was on the hunt "al-
    most every night": Donald Trump and Tony Schwartz,
    Trump: The Art of the Deal (New York: Ballantine, 2015), p. 97.

33 By Trump's account, Cohn became a business mentor
    and nearly a second father to him: Michael Kruse, "'He
    Brutalized For You.'" Politico. N.p., April 8, 2016. Web.
    June 16, 2016.

33   It also ensnared Trump in a jewelry tax scam and in a lawsuit: William Bastone, "The Bulgari Sales Tax Scam." *Village Voice*, November 25, 1986. Accessed June 20, 2016.

34   In Cohn, Trump had someone who could be "vicious" on his behalf: Kruse, "'He Brutalized For You.'"

34   Then he set out to join Le Club, which Trump regarded as "the hottest club in the city": Anthony Haden, "Donald Trump's Nights Out with Roy Cohn." *Daily Beast*, N.p., January 30, 2016. Web. June 5, 2016.

34   "I don't kid myself about Roy": Trump and Schwartz, *Trump: The Art of the Deal*, p. 99.

34   Fred Trump had faced similar accusations two decades earlier, both from the government and from legendary folk singer Woody Guthrie: Michael D'Antonio, "Ike Didn't Like Donald Trump's Dad." *Daily Beast*, N.p., November 23, 2015. Web. June 7, 2016.

34   Guthrie had moved into an apartment at Beach Haven, Fred Trump's first major housing project, in 1950: William Kaufman, "Woody Guthrie, 'Old Man Trump' and a Real Estate Empire's Racist Foundations." *The Conversation*, January 21, 2016. Accessed June 5, 2016. the-conversation.com/woody-guthrie-old-man-trump-and-a-real-estate-empires-racist-foundations-53026.

36   At Trump's Shore Haven apartments, the superintendent told a white woman: Gideon Resnick, "DOJ: Trump's Early Businesses Blocked Blacks." *Daily Beast*, December 15, 2015. Accessed June 8, 2016.

36   The Justice Department sued Donald Trump, his fa-

ther, and Trump Management: Morris Kaplan, "Major Landlord Accused of Antiblack Bias in City." *New York Times*, October 16, 1973. Accessed June 8, 2016.

36 But Donald Trump sought advice from Cohn: Kaplan, "Major Landlord Accused of Antiblack Bias in City."

36 Trump wrote that he told Cohn, "I don't like lawyers": Trump and Schwartz, *Trump: The Art of the Deal*, pp. 98–99.

37 Two months after this supposed first conversation with Cohn, Trump held a press conference at the New York Hilton: Michael Kranish and Robert O'Harrow Jr., "Inside the Government's Racial Bias Case Against Donald Trump's Company, and How He Fought It." *Washington Post*, January 23, 2016. Accessed June 9, 2016.

37 Cohn filed a lawsuit demanding $100 million in damages from the federal government: Barbara Campbell, "Realty Company Asks $100-Million 'Bias' Damages." *New York Times*, December 13, 1973. Accessed June 7, 2016.

37 The government's lawsuit and Trump's countersuit were heard in federal court in Brooklyn: Kranish and O'Harrow Jr., "Inside the Government's Racial Bias Case Against Donald Trump's Company, and How He Fought It." See also Wayne Barrett, *Trump: The Deals and the Downfall*, pp. 86–88.

38 In *The Art of the Deal*, Trump said he told Cohn: Trump and Schwartz, *Trump: The Art of the Deal*, p. 98.

38 A government press release heralded the settlement as "one of the most far reaching ever": Kruse, "'He Brutalized for You.'"

38 The settlement was a complete loss for Trump, but he spun the case as a massive win: Donald Trump and Tony Schwartz, *Trump: The Art of the Deal*, p. 99, and Wayne Barrett, *Trump: The Deals and the Downfall*, pp. 86–88.

38 The government routinely lets people who settle get off without admitting to any wrongdoing: Kruse, "'He Brutalized for You.'"

39 Even if he privately disagreed, or if pursuing a case was not in Cohn's best interest: Trump and Schwartz, *Trump: The Art of the Deal*, p. 100.

39 Among Cohn's other clients were two of America's most powerful Mafia figures: Albin Krebs, "Roy Cohn, Aide to McCarty and Fiery Lawyer, Dies at 59." *New York Times*, August 3, 1986: n. pag. Web. June 8, 2016.

CHAPTER 6. TRUMP'S MOST IMPORTANT DEALS

41 In *The Art of the Deal*, Trump boasts that when he applied for a casino owner's license: Donald Trump and Tony Schwartz, *Trump: The Art of the Deal* (New York: Ballantine, 2015), p. 210.

42 Trump set about arranging special terms to prevent scrutiny of his past: Trump and Schwartz, *Trump: The Art of the Deal*, p. 208.

42 Trump asked John Degnan, the New Jersey attorney general, to come to him: Trump and Schwartz, *Trump: The Art of the Deal*, p. 208.

42 He did not promise approval, but did promise that, if

Trump cooperated: Trump and Schwartz, *Trump: The Art of the Deal*, p. 207.

43 Of course, Trump was not clean as a whistle by the standards of: "Trump Thought A.C. Venture Could Tarnish Name." *The Smoking Gun*, March 30, 2004. Accessed June 9, 2016. www.thesmokinggun.com/documents/crime/trump-thought-ac-venture-could-tarnish-name.

43 In 1980, John Martin—the United States Attorney in Manhattan—briefly investigated: Tim Robbins, "The Truth About Trump and the Mob." *Newsweek*, May 1, 2016. See also David Cay Johnston, "Just What Were Donald Trump's Ties to the Mob." *Poltico*, May 22, 2016. Accessed June 8, 2016. www.politico.com/magazine/story/2016/05/donald-trump-2016-mob-organized-crime-213910.

44 The fourth case was the Justice Department's 1973 suit accusing Trump of racial discrimination: Morris Kaplan, "Major Landlord Accused of Antilock Bias in City." *New York Times*, October 16, 1973. Accessed June 8, 2016.

45 After completing its investigation of Trump in a record five months: David Cay Johnston, "Just What Were Donald Trump's Ties to the Mob." *Poltico*, May 22, 2016. See also David Cay Johnston, "Book Alleges Trump Did Business with Mob." *Philadelphia Inquirer*, January 7, 1992. Accessed June 6, 2016.

45 The reporter who broke the story, Wayne Barrett, was questioned by the DGE as part of the application investigation: Marcus Baram, "State Investigation Report on Trump Shows Complexity of Alleged Mob Ties."

Fast Company, March 7, 2016. Accessed June 9, 2016. www.fastcompany.com/3057495/state-investigative-report-on-trump-shows-complexity-of-alleged-mob-ties.

45 **The DGE gave Trump a pass on his failure to disclose:** Wayne Barrett, *Trump: The Deals and the Downfall*. See also **Johnston,** *Temples of Chance*, **p. 83.**

45 **It was an early sign of what two Casino Control commissioners:** Johnston, "Just What Were Donald Trump's Ties to the Mob."

46 **At the top, the mob controlled the unions and rigged their elections:** Arnold H. Lubasch, "U.S. Jury Convicts Eight as Members of Mob Commission." *New York Times*, November 20, 1986. Accessed June 8, 2016.

46 **S & A charged the inflated prices that the LeFrak and Resnik families complained about:** Selwyn Raab, "Irregularities in Concrete Industry Inflate Building Costs, Experts Say." *New York Times*, April 26, 1982. Accessed June 7, 2016.

46 **With Cohn as his fixer, Trump had no worries that the Mafia bosses would have the unions stop work:** Albin Krebs, "Roy Cohn, Aide to McCarty and Fiery Lawyer, Dies at 59." *New York Times*, August 3, 1986: Web. June 8, 2016. www.nytimes.com/library/national/science/aids/080386sci-aids.html.

47 **He denied meeting Salerno. Case closed:** Johnston, "Book Alleges Trump Did Business with Mob."

47 **Just as revealing was Trump's association with John Cody, the corrupt head of the Teamsters Local 282:** Johnston, "Just What Were Donald Trump's Ties to the Mob."

48 Trump, who insists in his presidential campaign that he never settles lawsuits: Tim Robbins, "The Truth About Trump and the Mob." *Newsweek*, May 1, 2016.

48 The chief trial prosecutor, Michael Chertoff, told the judge that the defendants: Johnston, "Just What Were Donald Trump's Ties to the Mob."

48 In 1988, Trump made a deal to put his name on Trump Golden Series and Trump Executive Series limousines: William Bastone, "Trump Limos Were Built With a Hood Ornament." *Smoking Gun*, September 22, 2015. Accessed June 8, 2016. www.thesmokinggun.com/documents/celebrity/trump-and-staluppi-092157.

CHAPTER 7. "A GREAT LAWSUIT"

51 Erecting gaudy buildings did not bring Donald Trump the national attention he craved: Ira Berkow, "Trump Building the Generals in His Own Style." *New York Times*, January 1, 1984.

52 Applying his P. T. Barnum–like skills at attracting attention: Drew Jubera, "How Donald Trump Destroyed a Football League." *Esquire*, January 13, 2016.

53 To promote the team, Trump sent the Brig-A-Dears to bars: Katz, Emily Tess, "Lisa Edelstein On Being a Cheerleader for Trump's Football Team: He Treated Them 'Like Hookers.'" *Huffington Post*, December 3, 2015. www.huffingtonpost.com/entry/lisa-edelstein-on-being-a-cheerleader-for-trumps-football-team-he-treated-them-like-hookers_us_56609e3de4b079b2818db65d.

53 Signing top college players and luring several pros

away from the NFL: UPI, "Trump Asks Help in Paying Flutie." *New York Times*, April 2, 1985.

53   None of this was consistent with Dixon's low-risk, low-cost plan: Ben Terris, "And Then There Was the Time Donald Trump Bought a Football Team . . ." *Washington Post*, October 19, 2015.

53   In 1984, Trump persuaded the other USFL owners to sue the NFL under the Sherman Antitrust Act: Lois Romano, "Donald Trump, Holding All the Cards The Tower! The Team! The Money! The Future!" *Washington Post*, November 15, 1984.

54   As the two men announced the lawsuit on October 18, 1984, Cohn said: Michael Janofsky, "Charges Fly from U.S.F.L." *New York Times*, October 19, 1984.

54   For the trial, Trump convinced the other USFL team owners to hire Harvey D. Myerson: Drew Jubera, "How Donald Trump Destroyed a Football League." *Esquire*, January 13, 2016.

55   After five days of deliberation, the jury found that the NFL had indeed engaged in criminal behavior: Jubera, "How Donald Trump Destroyed a Football League."

55   They awarded the USFL damages in the amount of one dollar: Jubera, "How Donald Trump Destroyed a Football League."

56   Myerson (who later spent seventy months in prison for tax evasion): Arnold H. Lubasch, "70 Months for Lawyer in Tax Fraud." *New York Times*, November 14, 1992.

56   "The jury found that the failure of the USFL was not

the result of the NFL's television contracts": Joe Nocera, "Donald Trump's Less-Than-Artful Failure in Pro Football." *New York Times*, February 19, 2016

57 "It would have been small potatoes," Trump says as he pulls off his microphone and walks out: Jubera, "How Donald Trump Destroyed a Football League."

57 Tollin extended Trump a courtesy in 2009 by sending him a rough cut of the film: Jubera, "How Donald Trump Destroyed a Football League."

CHAPTER 8. SHOWING MERCY

59 He piloted boats named *Mighty Mouse* and *Nuts 'n Bolts* in races off the Florida coast: William Bastone, "Trump Vouched for Cocaine Dealer." *The Smoking Gun*, February 16, 2016. Accessed June 7, 2016. www.thesmoking-gun.com/documents/celebrity/the-donald-and-the-dealer-173892.

60 At the time, Weichselbaum was already a twice-convicted felon: Bastone, "Trump Vouched for Cocaine Dealer."

60 Weichselbaum and his younger brother, Franklin: John Connolly, "Pal Joey." *Spy Magazine*, June 1991.

61 Why did Trump Plaza continue to pay $100,000 per month and Trump's Castle $80,000 a month: David Cay Johnston, "Just What Were Donald Trump's Ties to the Mob." *Politico*, May 22, 2016. Accessed May 26, 2016. www.politico.com/magazine/story/2016/05/don-ald-trump-2016-mob-organized-crime-213910.

61 Even though he had officially left the twice-failed heli-
    copter company, Weichselbaum: Tom Robbins, "Ex-
    Con Tied to Aycee Firm." The Marshall Project, April
    27, 2016. Accessed June 12, 2016. www.themarshallproj-
    ect.org/documents/2815164-Ex-con-tied-to-Aycee-firm#.
    Bef4Al4iK.

62 In addition to his helicopter business, Joey Weichsel-
    baum was an officer at a used-car dealership: William
    Bastone, "Trump Vouched for Cocaine Dealer."

63 Weichselbaum's Ohio lawyer, Arnold Morelli, sought
    in a January 30, 1986, motion: United States vs. Joseph
    Weichsebaum. Case no. CR 1. 85-108 Defendant's Mo-
    tion to Transfer

64 Trump characterized the defendant as "a credit to the
    community": Wayne Barrett, Trump: The Deals and the
    Downfall (New York: HarperCollins, 1992), p. 204.

64 Two years later, the DGE had to explain: (NJ) Division
    of Gaming Enforcement to the Casino Control Com-
    mission, Supplemental Report on the Qualifications of
    Donald J. Trump. December 1, 1992.

65 When he was up for early release, Weichselbaum told
    his parole offcer that he already had work lined up:
    Wayne Barrett, Trump: The Deals and the Downfall, p.
    204.

65 Weischselbaum also told his probation officer that he
    had known about Marla Maples: David Cay Johnston,
    "Book Alleges Trump Did Business with Mob." Philadel-
    phia Inquirer, January 7, 1992.

CHAPTER 9. POLISH BRIGADE

69   **Bonwit's twelve-story façade was adorned with a pair of giant bas-relief panels:** Christopher Gray, "The Store That Slipped Through the Cracks." *New York Times*, October 3, 2014.

69   **Trump assured those worried about the architectural treasures:** Robert D. McFadden, "Developer Scraps Bonwit Sculptures." *New York Times*, June 6, 1980.

70   **Instead of hiring an experienced demolition contractor:** Constance L. Hayes, "Judge Says Trump Tower Builders Cheated Union on Pension Funds." *New York Times*, April 27, 1991.

70   **They lacked facemasks, even though asbestos— known to cause incurable cancers—swirled all around them:** Selwyn Raab, "After 15 Years in Court, Workers' Lawsuit Against Trump Faces Yet Another Delay." *New York Times*, June 14, 1998.

70   **Trump kept an eye on the project, not just when visiting the site:** Dunstan Prial, "Before Running for President, Donald Trump's First Gamble Was Building Trump Tower." *Hollywood Reporter*, April 6, 2016. Accessed June 8, 2016. www.hollywoodreporter.com/features/before-running-president-donald-trumps-880084.

70   **The demolition workers were not American citizens:** Michael Daly, "Trump Tower Was Built on Undocumented Immigrants' Backs." *Daily Beast*, August 7, 2015. Accessed June 10, 2016. www.thedailybeast.com/articles/2015/07/08/trump-tower-was-built-on-undocumented-immigrants-backs.html.

70   Many members of the demolition crew, which became
     known as the Polish Brigade: Constance L. Hayes,
     "Judge Says Trump Tower Builders Cheated Union on
     Pension Funds."

70   sleeping through the bitter cold on bare concrete
     floors: Daly, "Trump Tower Was Built on Undocu-
     mented Immigrants' Backs."

71   "Donald told me he was having some difficulties," Sul-
     livan later testified: David Cay Johnston, "Just What
     Were Donald Trump's Ties to the Mob." *Politico.*

71   "Men were stripping electric wires with their bare
     hands," Sullivan later tesified: *Trump: What's the Deal?*
     Directed by Libby Handross. trumpthemovie.com.

72   Shortly after Trump called Sullivan, a new demolition
     crew arrived on the site: Selwyn Raab, "After 15 Years
     in Court, Workers' Lawsuit Against Trump Faces Yet
     Another Delay."

73   One day, to keep the workers swinging their sledge-
     hammers: Hardy v. Kaszycki & Sons Contractors, Inc.

73   After the building was taken down, a dissident mem-
     ber of the Housewreckers Union: Raab, "After 15 Years
     in Court, Workers' Lawsuit Against Trump Faces Yet
     Another Delay."

73   Judge Stewart, in a lengthy opinion, found that Trump's
     testimony lacks credibility: Hayes, "Judge Says Trump
     Tower Builders Cheated Union on Pension Funds."

73   Judge Stewart ruled that Trump had engaged in a con-
     spiracy to cheat the workers of their pay: Wayne Bar-
     rett, *Trump: The Deals and the Downfall,* p. 192.

74 There was no litigation over the destruction of the bas-relief façades: Robert D. McFadden, "Developer Scraps Bonwit Sculptures." *New York Times*, June 6, 1980.

75 Trump spoke up days later, saying safety concerns were his real worry: Robert D. McFadden, "Builder Says Costs Forced Scrapping of Bonwit Art; Three-Week Delay." *New York Times*, June 9, 1980.

CHAPTER 10. FEELINGS AND NET WORTH

77 In 1990, when his business empire was on the verge of collapse: David Cay Johnston, "Bankers Say Trump May Be Worth Less Than Zero." *Philadelphia Inquirer*, August 16, 1990. articles.philly.com/1990-08-16/news/25932770_1_donald-trump-trump-assets-trump-princess.

77 Just how does Trump arrive at these fluctuating figures?: Peter S. Goodman, "Trump Suit Claiming Defamation Is Dismissed." *New York Times*, July 15, 2009.

79 "I would say it's my general attitude at the time that the question may be asked": Trump vs. Timothy L. O'Brien, et al. No. CAM-L-545-06. Superior Court of New Jersey.

80 "I asked the client to provide me with a list of liabilities": Donald Trump v. Timothy L. O'Brien Superior Court of New Jersey, Appellate Division Docket NO. A-6141-08T3 Decided 9/7/2001.

81 Trump said he paid cash for the property, which he described as run-down: Donald Trump and Tony Schwartz, *Trump: The Art of the Deal* (New York: Ballantine, 2015), p. 26.

82   In December 1985, Trump had written to Janet VB
     Pena: Donald J. Trump to Janet VB Pena, Chase Man-
     hattan Bank. December 9, 1985. New York, New York.

82   The bank loaned Trump $2 million more than the pur-
     chase price: Chase Manhattan Bank to Donald J.
     Trump. November 26, 1985. New York, New York.

82   He boasted that he got Mar-a-Lagofor a song: Trump
     and Schwartz, *Trump: The Art of the Deal*, p. 26.

CHAPTER II. GOVERNMENT RESCUES TRUMP

85   His recorded cash flow averaged $1.6 million per week
     for 233 weeks: David Cay Johnston, *Temples of Chance:
     How America Inc. Bought out Murder Inc. to Win Control of
     the Casino Business* (New York: Doubleday, 1992), p. 231.

85   How could a man who had convinced the world he
     was a multibillionaire fail to pay contractors: Da-
     vid Cay Johnston, "Donald Trump's Bankruptcy
     Dodge: This Is How Lawyers and Regulators Helped
     Him Fudge Solvency and Avoid Collapse." *Salon*,
     April 30, 2016. www.salon.com/2016/04/30/donald_
     trumps_bankruptcy_dodge_this_is_how_lawyers_
     and_regulators_helped_him_fudge_solvency_and_
     avoid_collapse/.

86   Trump's inability to pay his debts had put him at risk:
     David Cay Johnston, *Temples of Chance: How America Inc.
     Bought out Murder Inc. to Win Control of the Casino Busi-
     ness.* Pg 233

86   At the time, Trump told me and everybody else that
     he was worth $3 billion: David Cay Johnston, "The Art

of the Inside Deal." *Washington Spectator*, April 25, 2016. washingtonspectator.org/trump-finance-regulators/.

87 **A few weeks later, I got my hands on Trump's personal financial statement:** David Cay Johnston, "Bankers Say Trump May Be Worth Less Than Zero." *Philadelphia Inquirer*, August 16, 1990.

87 **Soon after that news story, casino regulators publicized a document:** Johnston, *Temples of Chance: How America Inc. Bought out Murder Inc. to Win Control of the Casino Business*, p. 232.

87 **Trump's obvious difficulty complying with the financial stability requirements:** Johnston, *Temples of Chance: How America Inc. Bought out Murder Inc. to Win Control of the Casino Business*, pp. 231 and 234.

88 **But Trump's unpaid bills and the presence of all those bankers in Trump Tower:** David Cay Johnston, "The Art of the Inside Deal."

88 **The seventy banks whose massive loans were about to sour insisted that Trump install a man: Steven F. Bollenbach:** Johnston, *Temples of Chance: How America Inc. Bought out Murder Inc. to Win Control of the Casino Business*, p. 230.

89 **"You may well be worth more than Donald Trump":** Johnston, "Bankers Say Trump May Be Worth Less Than Zero."

89 **Instead, the Casino Control Commision listened to a less than vigorous challenge:** Johnston, *Temples of Chance: How America Inc. Bought out Murder Inc. to Win Control of the Casino Business*, p. 232.

90 **The DGE prepared its own 111-page report:** Johnston, *Temples of Chance: How America Inc. Bought out Murder Inc. to Win Control of the Casino Business*, p. 231.

90 **Part of the deal was putting Trump on an allowance:** Kurt Eichenwald, "Quick: Who'd Have Trouble Living on $450,000 a Month?" *New York Times*, June 26, 1990.

91 **"Trump Empire Could Tumble Today, Casino Panel Told":** David Cay Johnston, "Trump Empire Could Tumble Today, Casino Panel Told." *Philadelphia Inquirer*, August 17, 1990.

93 **In the spring of 2016, Trump told CNBC:** Binyamin Appelbaum, "Donald Trump's Idea to Cut National Debt: Get Creditors to Accept Less." CNBC.COM. May 6, 2016. www.cnbc.com/2016/05/06/donald-trumps-idea-to-cut-national-debt-get-creditors-to-accept-less.html.

CHAPTER 12. GOLF AND TAXES

95 **Of Trump's fifteen golf courses:** Michael Bamberger, "Donald Trump Details His Golfing Ambitions, Dust-ups with Jack Nicklaus, the USGA and Golf Digest." Golf.com, August 19, 2011.

95 **Among Trump's top-valued properties is the Trump National Golf Club Westchester:** Trump National Golf Club Westchester. June 7, 2016. www.trumpnational-westchester.com/Default.aspx?p=dynamicmodule&pageid=100119&ssid=100132&vnf=1.

96 **Bill Clinton, who owns a home six miles away, is among those who have paid the club's initiation fee:** Shawn Tully, "Trump Once Said Some Amazing Things

About His Net Worth Under Oath." *Forbes*, March 3, 2016.

96   While Trump declared (also under oath) that more than $50 million: David Cay Johnston, "Donald Trump's Worthless Real Estate Math." *Daily Beast*, May 24, 2016. www.thedailybeast.com/articles/2016/05/24/donald-trump-s-worthless-real-estate-math.html.

96   The difference between what Trump swore in his Federal Election Commission filings: Mathew Mosk, Brian Ross, and Randy Kreider, "Trump Team Revises Golf Course Value Amid Tax Controversy." abcnews.Go.com. May 16, 2016. abcnews.go.com/Politics/trump-team-revises-golf-amid-tax-controversy/story?id=39155939.

97   Trump's appeal annoyed the locals: David McKay Wilson, "Trump Seeks 90% Tax Cut at New York Golf Club." *USA Today*, September 3, 2015.

97   According to court documents filed by Briarcliff Manor: David McKay Wilson, "Trump at War with Briarcliff Manor Over $238k Flood Bill." Lohud.com, September 11, 2015. www.lohud.com/story/money/personal-finance/taxes/david-mckay-wilson/2015/09/10/trump-war-briarcliff-manor-over-238k-flood-damage-bill/71950004/.

98   In the rolling open hills of Bedminster, New Jersey: Walter O'Brien, "Donald Trump Loves NYC, But Will Spend Eternity in Bedminster." Nj.com. September 26, 2013. www.nj.com/somerset/index.ssf/2013/09/donald_trump_may_love_new_york_but_hell_spend_eternity_in_bedminster.html.

98 For property tax purposes, assessors make separate determinations of value: Jon Swaine, "How Trump's $50m Golf Club Became $1.4m When It Came Time to Pay Tax." *Guardian*, March 12, 2016. www.theguardian.com/us-news/2016/mar/12/donald-trump-briarcliff-manor-golf-course-tax.

99 The property tax in 2015 was just under $440,000: Richard Rubin, "Goat Herd Helps Trump Lower Tax Bite." *Wall Street Journal*, April 20, 2016.

99 The Trump National Golf Club Los Angeles: Gene Maddaus, "Donald Trump's Palos Verdes Golf Course Has Holes in It." *Variety*, June 9, 2016.

99 Trump gained property tax and income tax breaks on the Palos Verdes property: Gene Maddaus, "Donald Trump's Palos Verdes Golf Course Has Holes in It."

100 Trump tried to develop the land anyway, only to be told no: Victoria Kim, "Trump Sues City for $100 Million." *Los Angeles Times*, December 20, 2008.

100 Showing his relish for litigation: Victoria Kim, "Trump Sues City for $100 Million."

101 On Trump's behalf, Alderman Burke won tax discounts: Tim Novak and Chris Fusco, "Watchdogs: The Donald & the Democrat; Burke Saved Trump $11. 7 Million." *Chicago Sun-Times*, April 30, 2016.

101 Kelly Keeling Hahn, a lawyer at Alderman Burke's firm: Novak Fusco, "Watchdogs: The Donald & the Democrat; Burke Saved Trump $11. 7 Million."

CHAPTER 13. INCOME TAXES

103 Mitnick has testified that he is "thoroughly familiar" with every aspect of Trump's finances: State of New York Division of Tax Appeals. In the Matter of the Petition of East 61st Street Company. Determination DTA NO. 811470

103 In *The Art of the Deal*, Trump recounts a typical conversation with Mitnick: Donald Trump and Tony Schwartz, *Trump: The Art of the Deal* (New York: Ballantine Books, 2015), p. 14.

103 Trump had done well following his accountant's advice: Chris Good and Ryan Struyk, "Donald Trump Twice Paid No Federal Taxes, Government Report Shows." ABC News, May 20, 2016. abcnews.go.com/Politics/donald-trump-paid-federal-taxes-government-report-shows/story?id=39259669.

104 Trump's 1978 tax return reported a negative income of $406,379: Associated Press. "Here's What Might Be Hiding in Donald Trump's Tax Returns." Fortune, May 12, 2016.

105 Trump's federal tax return included a Schedule C: David Cay Johnston, "New Evidence Donald Trump Didn't Pay Taxes." *Daily Beast*, June 15, 2016. www.thedailybeast.com/articles/2016/06/15/new-evidence-donald-trump-didn-t-pay-taxes.html.

106 Trump appealed. Mitnick argued his case: State of New York Division of Tax Appeals. In the Matter of the Petition of East 61st Street Company. Determination DTA NO. 811470.

106   "We did not" prepare that return, Mitnick testified:
      State of New York Division of Tax Appeals. In the Mat-
      ter of the Petition of East 61st Street Company. Determi-
      nation DTA NO. 811470.

107   Tillman found no factual basis for Trump's unsub-
      stantiated deductions: State of New York Division of
      Tax Appeals. In the Matter of the Petition of East 61st
      Street Company. Determination DTA NO. 811470.

108   Mitnick, again the sole witness for Trump: State of
      New York Division of Tax Appeals. In the Matter of the
      Petition of East 61st Street Company. Determination
      DTA NO. 811470.

108   The year 1984 was not the last time Trump paid no
      income tax: Shane Goldmacher, "Trump Appears to
      Have Paid No Taxes for Two Years in Early 1990s." Polit-
      ico, June 17, 2016. www.politico.com/story/2016/06/don-
      ald-trump-no-taxes-224498.

109   Let's take Trump at his word to illustrate how the tax
      system works: Kim Masters, "NBC Calls Donald
      Trump 'Apprentice' Salary Report 'Grossly Inaccurate.'"
      Hollywood Reporter, June 22, 2011. www.hollywoodre-
      porter.com/news/nbc-calls-donald-trump-apprentice-
      204698.

CHAPTER 14. EMPTY BOXES

111   It, too, was mailed out of state: William Bastone, "The
      Bulgari Sales Tax Scam." Village Voice, November 25,
      1986. Accessed June 20, 2016.

112   Bulgari had put an asterisk next to the name of every

customer who received an empty box: Kirk Johnson, "Bulgari Pleads Guilty in a a Sales-Tax Scheme." *New York Times*, December 6, 1986.

112 Trump was not the only customer named in the investigation: UPI. "Celebrities Listed as Buyers in Sales Tax Evasion Case." *Los Angeles Times*, November 20, 1986. Accessed June 16, 2016.

112 disclosures of the names of the customers under scrutiny: Kirk Johnson, "Bulgari Pleads Guilty in a Sales-Tax Scheme." *New York Times*, December 6, 1986.

112 The story was broken by William Bastone: William Bastone, "The Bulgari Sales Tax Scam." *Village Voice*, November 25, 1986. Accessed June 20, 2016.

113 The grand jury heard testimony regarding 202 instances: "THE CITY; Bulgari Official Listed as Fugitive." *New York Times*, August 9, 1985: n. pg. *New York Times*. Web. June 8, 2016.

113 Rubenstein said Trump had engaged only in "bona fide transactions": William Bastone, "The Bulgari Sales Tax Scam." *Village Voice*, November 25, 1986. Accessed June 20, 2016.

113 Robert Abrams, who was then the New York state attorney general: "THE CITY; Bulgari Official Listed as Fugitive." *New York Times*, August 9, 1985: n. pg. *New York Times*. Web. June 8, 2016.

114 "We should embarrass them," Koch said: Kirk Johnson, "Bulgari Pleads Guilty in a Sales-Tax Scheme." *New York Times*, December 6, 1986.

114 Khashoggi lost the boat when he could not pay his

creditors: William C. Rempel, "Latest Financial Set-back for Billionaire Saudi Arms Dealer: Sultan of Brunei Seizes Khashoggi Yacht." *Los Angeles Times*, May 15, 1987: n. pag. Web. June 12, 2016.

114   He then leased the ship to himself so that he only had to pay sales taxes on the monthly lease payments: AP. "Jersey Exempts Trump From Yacht Sales Tax." *New York Times*, September 21, 1988: n. pag. Web. June 12, 2016.

115   Trump's allies told *The New York Times* that he was about to sell the yacht for $110 million: Richard D. Hylton, "Trump Is Reportedly Selling Yacht." *New York Times*, May 11, 1990: n. pag. Web. June 6, 2016.

CHAPTER 15. "BETTER THAN HARVARD"

117   Michael Sexton, a management consultant and for-profit education entrepreneur: "Sonny Low J. R. Ever-ett, Et Al. vs Trump University." June 22, 2016. www.documentcloud.org/documents/2895623-Declara-tion-of-Jason-Forge-With-Exhibits.html.

118   First, there was no "university": Nick Gass, "New York AG: Trump U 'Really a Fraud from Beginning to End.'" *Politico*, June 2, 2016. www.politico.com/story/2016/06/eric-schneiderman-trump-university-fraud-223812.

118   no other address has as many unregistered stock bro-kerage firms: Zeke Faux and Max Abelson, "Inside Trump's Most Valuable Tower: Felons, Dictators and Girl Scouts." *Bloomberg*, June 22, 2016. www.bloomberg.com/graphics/2016-trump-40-wall-street/.

118 **One week after Trump University declared itself:** "Sonny Low J.R. Everett, et al. vs Trump University, et al." June 22, 2016. www.documentcloud.org/documents/2895623-Declaration-of-Jason-Forge-With-Exhibits.html.

118 **The faux university also did not have professors:** Steven Brill, "What the Legal Battle Over Trump University Reveals About Its Founder." *Time*, November 5, 2015.

119 **Trump did not even honor his commitment to handpick the faculty:** "Sonny Low J.R. Everett, et al. vs Trump University, et al."

119 **It is worth noting that Trump's memory seemed quite keen:** Katy Tur and Ali Vitali, "Amid Latest Controversy, Trump Claims 'World's Greatest Memory.'" NBC News, November 24, 2015. www.nbcnews.com/politics/2016-election/amid-latest-controversy-trump-claims-worlds-greatest-memory-n468621.

119 **when Jensen finally asked if Trumpcould name:** "Sonny Low J.R. Everett, et al. vs Trump University, et al."

120 **None of this was true either:** Lynn Walsh and J. W. August, "Transcripts of Donald Trump Depositions in Trump University Lawsuits Released." NBC San Diego. www.nbcsandiego.com/news/local/Transcripts-Of-Donald-Trump-Depositions-in-Trump-University-Lawsuits-Released-384157741.html.

120 **The testimony above all comes from a 2012 suit:** "Sonny Low J.R. Everett, et al. vs Trump University, et al."

121 What it actually offered was a list that traced back to the *Scotsman Guide*: "A. G. Schneiderman Sues Donald Trump, Trump University & Michael Sexton For Defrauding Consumers Out of $40 Million with Sham 'University.'" New York State Office of the Attorney General, August 25, 2013. www.ag.ny.gov/press-release/ ag-schneiderman-sues-donald-trump-trump-university -michael-sexton-defrauding-consumers.

121 Among the investigators' findings was that students who attended: Bill Chappell, "'Trump University' Documents Put on Display Aggressive Sales Techniques." NPR, May 31, 2016. www.npr.org/sections/thetwo-way /2016/05/31/480214102/trump-university-playbooks-released-by-court-advise-being-courteous-to-media.

121 The consumer protection investigators also reported: Patrick Svitek, "In Texas, Trump U Shut Down After State Scrutiny." *Texas Tribune*, June 2, 2016.

122 We know about all this because John Owens: Tom LoBianco and David Fitzpatrick, "Was Trump University Run Out of Texas or Let Go?" CNN, June 6, 2016. www .cnn.com/2016/06/06/politics/texas-trump-university/.

123 In 2013, three years after Berlin failed to persuade Abbott: Brian M. Rosenthal and Gabrielle Banks, "Inside the Probe into Trump University That Abbott's Office Launched and Then Ended." *Houston Chronicle*, June 2, 2016.

124 Both Bondi (a lawyer) and Trump would have known: Fred Grimm, "Donald Trump Buys Himself an Attorney General for $25,000." *Miami Herald*, June 8, 2016.

124 In fact, on the last day of June 2016: David Willman,

"FBI Interviews Hillary Clinton over Her Email Use While Secretary of State." *Los Angeles Times*, July 6, 2016.

124 **"Who would do this?" Trump demanded:** Louis Nelson, "Trump: Bill Clinton Meeting with Loretta Lynch 'So Horrible.'" *Politico*, June 30, 2016. www.politico.com/story/2016/06/trump-bill-clinton-loretta-lynch-meeting-224983.

125 **For both Trump and Bondi, the cashing of that check:** Greg Rohrer, "Lawyer Seeks Federal Bribery Charges against Bondi over Trump Donation." *Orlando Sentinel*, June 29, 2016.

126 **Allen Weisselberg:** David A. Fahrenthold and Rosiland S. Helderman, "Trump Camp Says $25,000 Charity Contribution to Florida AG Was a Mistake." *Washington Post*, March 22, 2016.

127 **The next day, Trump continued his attack on the judge's heritage:** Alan Rappeport, "That Judge Attacked by Donald Trump? He's Faced a Lot Worse." *New York Times*, June 3, 2016.

127 **The comments prompted the *National Review*:** Ian Tuttle, "Trump's Outrageous Attack on Judge Curiel." *National Review*, June 6, 2016.

CHAPTER 16. TRUMP CHARITIES

129 **"I told them it would endanger our status as a charitable organization":** David Cay Johnston, phone interview Keith Howard. June 10, 2016.

129 **He was right:** Tim Mak, "Exclusive: Trump Tried to

Pay Vets to Be Props." *Daily Beast*, February 6, 2016. www.thedailybeast.com/articles/2016/02/06/nh-vets-pass-on-being-trump-s-paid-props.html.

130 **Eventually Liberty House did get the promised money:** Johnston, phone interview Howard. June 10, 2016.

130 **During another campaign event in Iowa, less than two weeks:** Tim Mak, "Trump Vets Chair: Charity Money? Not My Problem." *Daily Beast*, April 22, 2016. www.thedailybeast.com/articles/2016/04/22/trump-vets-chair-charity-money-not-my-problem.html.

130 **Four months passed with no evidence that any money had been distributed:** Michael Bisecker, Jill Colvin, and Steven Peoples, "Big Trump Checks to Vets Groups Sent on Day of Media Report." Associated Press, May 31, 2016. bigstory.ap.org/article/44c48343f6244ea58768180a94d09429/trump-detail-fund-raising-veterans-charities.

130 **"The press should be ashamed of themselves," Trump said:** Jeremy Diamond, "Trump Launches All-out Attack on the Press." CNN, June 1, 2016. www.cnn.com/2016/05/31/politics/donald-trump-veterans-announcement/.

CHAPTER 17. IMAGINARY FRIENDS

135 **After the destruction of the Bonwit Teller building:** Robert D. McFadden, "Designer Astonished by Loss of Bonwitt Grillwork." *New York Times*, June 8, 1980.

135 **For years, Trump telephoned journalists using the name John Baron (or Barron):** David Cay Johnston,

"Trump Used His Aliases for Much More—And Worse—Than Gossip." *The National Memo*, May 14, 2016. Accessed May 14, 2016. www.nationalmemo.com /trump-used-aliases-much-more-worse-gossip/.

135   **He posed as a publicist, planting stories:** Tierney McAfee, "Donald Trump Denies He Masqueraded as His Own Publicist About Models, Madonna and Marla Maples." *People*, May 13, 2016.

135b **Then, using his own name, Trump confirmed what Baron had said:** UPI. "Trump Asks Help in Paying Flutie." *New York Times*, April 2, 1985.

136   **The deception began when Barron:** UPI. "Trump Asks Help in Paying Flutie." *New York Times*, April 2, 1985.

137   **For years, Trump planted stories:** vimeo.com/ondemand/trumpwhatsthedeal. See also Johnston, "Trump Used His Aliases For Much More—And Worse—Than Gossip."

138   **Handros's scathing 1991 film,** *Trump: What's the Deal?***:** David Cay Johnston, "Trump: Documentary the Donald Suppressed, Free at Last." *The National Memo*, August 1, 2015. Accessed June 5, 2016. www.nationalmemo .com/trump-documentary-the-donald-suppressed-free-at-last/. See also trumpthemovie.com/menu/#about.

CHAPTER 18. IMAGINARY LOVERS

139   **The unraveling of Trump's John Miller deception began with:** Eun Kyung Kim, "Donald Trump Denies Posing as Spokesman in Recordings *Washington Post* Uncovered." *Today News*, May 13, 2016. Accessed June 6,

2016. www.today.com/news/donald-trump-denies-posing-spokesman-recordings-washington-post-uncovered-t92421.

139 **Sue Carswell, a reporter:** Sue Carswell, "Trump Says Goodbye Marla, Hello Carla and a Mysterious PR Man Who Sounds Just like Donald Calls to Spread the Story." *People*, August 8, 1991.

141 **She told Trump that her sister would be joining her in New York:** Harry Hurt, *The Lost Tycoon: The Many Lives of Donald J. Trump* (New York: W. W. Norton, 1993), p. 386.

141 **"He's living with Marla and he's got three other girlfriends":** Sue Carswell, "Trump Says Goodbye Marla, Hello Carla and a Mysterious PR Man Who Sounds Just like Donald Calls to Spread the Story." *People*, August 8, 1991.

145 **"Trump is obviously a lunatic":** Michael Qazvini, "Former French First Lady and Fake Ex-Lover: 'Trump Is Obviously a Lunatic.'" *Daily Wire*, April 5, 2016. Accessed June 8, 2016. www.dailywire.com/news/4690/former-french-first-lady-and-fake-ex-lover-trump-michael-qazvini.

CHAPTER 19. MYTH MAINTENANCE

147 **"I spent a couple of bucks on legal fees":** Paul Farhi, "What Really Gets Under Trump's Skin? Questioning His Net Worth." *Washington Post*, March 8, 2016. www.washingtonpost.com/lifestyle/style/that-time-trump-sued-over-the-size-of-hiswallet/2016/03/08/785dee3e-e4c2-11e5-b0fd-073d5930a7b7_story.html.

148 **On a Friday morning, Trump called NBC's** *Today Show*: Marc Fisher, "In 1991 Interview, Trump Spokesman Sounds a Lot Like Trump." *Washington Post*, May 12, 2016.

148 **"No, I don't know anything about it"**: Eun Kyung Kim, "Donald Trump Denies Posing as Spokesman in Recordings *Washington Post* Uncovered." *Today News*, May 13, 2016. www.today.com/news/donald-trump-denies-posing-spokesman-recordings-washington-post-uncovered-t92421.

149 **"*No*, and it was not me on the phone"**: Kim, "Donald Trump Denies Posing as Spokesman in Recordings *Washington Post* Uncovered."

149 **Hours later, Katrina Pierson**: Situation Room, transcript. "Trump Denies Posing as His Own Spokesman." CNN, May 13, 2016. www.cnn.com/TRANSCRIPTS/1605/13/sitroom.01.html.

150 **The last option would seem unavailable to Trump**: Katy Tur and Ali Vitali, "Amid Latest Controversy, Trump Claims 'World's Greatest Memory.'" nbcnews.com, November 24, 2015. www.nbcnews.com/politics/2016-election/amid-latest-controversy-trump-claims-worlds-greatest-memory-n468621.

150 **Trump's emphatic** *Today Show* **denials left no escape hatch**: Callum Borchers, "Trump Claims He Didn't Regularly Use a Fake Name. That's Not What He Said Under Oath." *Washington Post*, May 13, 2016.

150 **The success of Trump's strategy was illustrated**: "Donald Trump Denies Posing as His Spokesman." CBS Evening News, May 13, 2016. www.cbsnews

.com/videos/donald-trump-denies-posing-as-his-own-spokesperson/.

151 On the *Today Show*, Trump employed another of his strategies: Kim, "Donald Trump Denies Posing as Spokesman in Recordings *Washington Post* Uncovered."

152 Had Carswell wanted to make news: "Big News? Trump Posed as PR Man; Plus, Megyn Kelly's Trump Truce." FoxNews.com, May 15, 2016. www.foxnews .com/transcript/2016/05/15/big-news-trump-posed-as-pr-man-plus-megyn-kelly-trump-truce/.

CHAPTER 20. COLLECTING HONORS

155 Trump International Golf Links: Trump Golf Scotland. Accessed June 8, 2016. www.trumpgolfscotland .com/awards.

155 The American Academy of Hospitality Sciences holds its honors: "Trump Acquaintance 'Joey No Socks' Helms Firm That Lavished Awards on Trump Businesses." *Tribune News Service*, May 20, 2016.

155 At the 2014 Mar-a-Lago New Year's Eve party, Cinque presented Trump: Hunter Walker, "How a Convicted Felon Nicknamed 'Joey No Socks' Covered Donald Trump in Stars." *Yahoo News*, May 20, 2016.

156 For years, those trustees included none other than Donald J. Trump: Walker, "How a Convicted Felon Nicknamed 'Joey No Socks' Covered Donald Trump in Stars."

157 A majority of the trustess bestowing these awards on

Trump: Walker, "How a Convicted Felon Nicknamed 'Joey No Socks' Covered Donald Trump in Stars."

157 **Another trustee was Anthony Senecal:** David Corn, "On Facebook, Trump's Longtime Butler Calls for Obama to Be Killed." *Mother Jones*, May 12, 2016. www.motherjones.com/politics/2016/05/trump-butler-anthony-senecal-facebook-kill-obama.

157 **Senecal, decked out in formal butler attire:** Walker, "How a Convicted Felon Nicknamed 'Joey No Socks' Covered Donald Trump in Stars."

157 **In his role as ambassador extraordinaire:** *Tribune News Service*, "Trump Acquaintance 'Joey No Socks' Helms Firm That Lavished Awards on Trump Businesses."

158 **Cinque is known by other names:** John Connolly, "The Preppy Don." *New York Magazine*, April 17, 1995.

158 **Gotti told Clinque that he would:** Connolly, "The Preppy Don."

158 **Clinque described himself very differently:** Connolly, "The Preppy Don."

159 **In addition to whatever stolen goods fencing or drug dealing:** Walker, "How a Convicted Felon Nicknamed 'Joey No Socks' Covered Donald Trump in Stars."

159 **He told the Associated Press that he hardly knows Cinque:** *Tribune News Service*, "Trump Acquaintance 'Joey No Socks' Helms Firm That Lavished Awards on Trump Businesses."

160 **As for his children and employees being trustees:** Walker, "How a Convicted Felon Nicknamed 'Joey No Socks' Covered Donald Trump in Stars."

160   "If a guy's going to give you an award": *Tribune News
       Service*, "Trump Acquaintance 'Joey No Socks' Helms
       Firm That Lavished Awards on Trump Businesses."

CHAPTER 21. WHO'S THAT?

161   Rebchook also questioned Trump's nattily dressed
       traveling companion: Charles V. Bagli, "Real Estate Ex-
       ecutive with Hand in Trump Projects Rose from Tan-
       gled Past." *New York Times*, December 17, 2007.

162   "Satter's" name appears with just one T in a host of
       places: Ben Mathis-Lilley, "Oh Look, Another Violent
       Psycho With Close Ties to Donald Trump." *Slate*, April
       6, 2016. www.slate.com/blogs/the_slatest/2016/04/06
       /donald_trump_and_felix_sater_felon.html

162   The name Sater with one *T* also appears on federal
       court papers: Bagli, "Real Estate Executive with Hand
       in Trump Projects Rose from Tangled Past."

162   Donald Trump, the Trump Organization, and Alan
       Garten: Bagli, "Real Estate Executive with Hand in
       Trump Projects Rose from Tangled Past."

163   When Sater left Bayrock, he moved into the Trump
       Organization suite of offices: Jeff Horwitz, Associated
       Press. "Donald Trump Picked Stock Fraud Felon as
       Senior Advisor." *Washington Times*, December 4, 2015.
       www.washingtontimes.com/news/2015/dec/4/donald-
       trump-picked-felix-sater-stock-fraud-felon-/.

164   "Purchasers had a right to know who they were deal-
       ing with," Altschul said: Michael Sallah, "High Court

Reveals Secret Deal of Trump Developer's Crimes." *Miami Herald*, July 31, 2012.

164 **"On this one, they got very, very fortunate that they didn't put their money down":** Michael Sallah and Michael Vasquez, "Failed Donald Trump Tower Thrust into GOP Campaign for Presidency." *Miami Herald*, March 12, 2016.

165 **According to Lauria—and the court files that have been unsealed:** Michael Sallah, "Strange Bedfellows: Swindler, Stiger-missle Brokers, the CIA." *Miami Herald*, September 10, 2012.

165 **Yet when the Associated Press asked about Sater in 2015:** Rosalind S. Helderman and Tom Hamburger, "Former Mafia-Linked Figure Describes Association with Trump."

CHAPTER 22. DOWN MEXICO WAY

168 **Prospective buyers were given:** Michael Finnegan, "Trump's Failed Baja Condo Resort Left Buyers Feeling Betrayed and Angry." *Los Angeles Times*, June 27, 2016. The promises, newsletters, and other events drawn from O'Brien v. Trump and related cases consolidated as Judicial Coordinating Coordination Proceeding No. 4642.

168 **Ivanka Trump told sales reception attendees:** Michael Finnegan, "Trump's Failed Baja Condo Resort Left Buyers Feeling Betrayed and Angry."

169 **Nearly two hundred people bought in:** Kaitlin Ugolik,

"Developer Pays $7M to Settle Suit Over Trump Mexico Resort." LAW360.com. October 4, 2012. www.law360.com/articles/384254/developer-pays-7m-to-settle-suit-over-trump-mexico-resort.

169 A June 2007 newsletter notified buyers that construction was underway: Michael Finnegan, "Trump's Failed Baja Condo Resort Left Buyers Feeling Betrayed and Angry."

169 "From the desk of Ivanka Trump": David K. Randall, "Trouble for Donald Trump: The Money for a Condo Project Didn't Come Through." *Forbes*, October 29, 2008.

170 The actual Baja developers, it came out later: Stuart Pfeifer, "Donald Trump Settles Lawsuit over Baja Condo Resort That Went Bust." *Los Angeles Times*, November 27, 2013.

171 He also declared under oath in those cases: Deposition of Donald J. Trump. CASE NO. BC409651, Superior Court of California. County of Los Angeles, Central District.

171 Trump in fact owned real estate in California: Steve Aaron, et al v. The Trump Organization, et al. United States District Court. Middle District of Florida, Tampa Division. No.8:09-CV-2493.

172 "More importantly," the Trump lawyers continued: Opposition to Motion for Order Determining "Good Faith" Settlement. Judicial Council Coordination Proceeding NO. 4642. Superior Court of California. County of Los Angeles, Central Civil West Courthouse

173 **The only duty the Trump parties had:** Opposition to Motion for Order Determining "Good Faith" Settlement. Judicial Council Coordination Proceeding NO. 4642.

173 **The court sealed the terms of the settlement:** Pfeifer, "Donald Trump Settles Lawsuit over Baja Condo Resort That Went Bust."

173 **Trump boasted that the combination of his name and Waikiki:** "Donald J. Trump and Irongate Announce Plans for Luxury Hotel-Condominiums at Waikiki Beach Walk; Trump Tower Waikiki Includes Hotel-Condos, Retail and Dining." *Business Wire*, May 31, 2006. www.businesswire.com/news/home/2006053 1006182/en/Donald-J.-Trump-Irongate-Announce-Plans -Luxury.

173 **On page twenty-three of the brochure:** "Trump Tower Might Not Really Be a Trump." *Star Bulletin* (Honolulu), July 14, 2009. archives.starbulletin.com/content/2009 0714_Trump_Tower_might_not_really_be_a_Trump.

174 **And in another Florida case:** Natalie Rodriguez, "Condole Buyers Want Previous Trump Testimony On Record." LAW360.com. December 10, 2013. www.law360 .com/articles/494613/condotel-buyers-want-previous- trump-testimony-on-record.

174 **In the Tampa case, Trump was asked about disclosures:** Steve Aaron, et al v. The Trump Organization, et al. United States District Court. Middle District of Florida, Tampa Division. No. 8:09-CV-2493.

175 **Those buyers received a sales brochure:** Drew Griffin,

Nelli Black, and Curt Devine, "Buying a Trump? Better Read the Fine Print." CNN, February 22, 2016. www .cnn.com/2016/02/22/politics/trump-properties-investigation/.

175 **The project failed and buyers wanted their deposits back:** Shaun Bevan, "Jury Sides with Donald Trump in Fort Lauderdale Condo Lawsuit." *South Florida Business Journal*, May 14, 2014. www.bizjournals.com/southflorida/blog/2014/03/jury-sides-with-donald-trump-in-fort-lauderdale.html.

CHAPTER 23. TRUMP BEACHES A WHALE

See my first book, *Temples of Chance* (Doubleday, 1992), for additional information on Trump's relationship with Kashiwagi. This chapter's sources are found in that work and Kashiwagi's obituaries in Japanese newspapers.

CHAPTER 24. BIGGEST LOSER

For sources and additional information of Trump's and Libutti's complex, and at time tenuous, relationship, please see my 1992 book, *Temples of Chance* (Doubleday).

INDEX

ABOUT THE AUTHOR

DAVID CAY JOHNSTON is an investigative journalist and winner of a 2001 Pulitzer Prize for journalism.
A longtime reporter for *The New York Times* and the former
president of Investigative Reporters and Editors (IRE), he
is also the author of several *New York Times* bestsellers,
including *Perfectly Legal* and *Free Lunch*. He has won the
IRE Medal and a George Polk Award for his investigative
reporting, and is a columnist for *The Daily Beast*, *The National Memo*, *Tax Notes*, and *USA Today*. Johnston lectures
widely on economics, journalism, and tax policy. He
teaches at Syracuse University College of Law and lives in
Rochester, New York.